EXPLOI
OXFORD....

*Discover the secrets of Oxfordshire
with 10 original tours and unusual places to visit*

Irene Boston

S.B. Publications

By the same author:
100 Walks in Warwickshire and West Midlands
Strolls and Walks from Midland Villages
Town and Village Discovery Trails — Warwickshire
Secrets of Worcestershire
A Worcestershire Quiz Book
A Warwickshire Quiz Book

First published in 1998 by S. B. Publications
c/o 19 Grove Road, Seaford, East Sussex BN25 1TP

ISBN 1 85770 164 X

Typeset and printed by:
MFP Design & Print,
Longford Trading Estate, Thomas Street, Stretford, Manchester M32 0KT

CONTENTS

Front cover: View to Little Wittenham from path to Wittenham
Clumps, near river Thames.

Back cover: Carved figures, tomb of Alice, Duchess of Suffolk,
St Mary's church, Ewelme.

Title page: Cottages, High Street, Burford.

INTRODUCTION

To some modern visitors, Oxfordshire means one of two things - the morning coach stop at Blenheim Palace or Inspector Morse. This limited perception is a great pity, for the county has much to offer, as any exploration beyond the obvious tourist attractions soon demonstrates.

A journey through Oxfordshire reveals a tremendous variety of scenery. The gentle hills of the north and west owe much to the nearby Cotswolds. South of Oxford lie the North Wessex Downs and the Vale of the White Horse, an area redolent of the past. The chalk downland, deep combes and woodlands of the Chilterns form a barrier to London's home counties. Slicing the county in two, our mightiest river, the Thames, has always been a vital artery, transporting people and goods towards London. Its tributaries, the Evenlode, Windrush, Cherwell and Thame, meander through lush corridors across farmland. The plain around Banbury and the clay of the Oxford vale offer a tranquil contrast to the rolling downland further south.

Berkshire may still be licking its wounds following surgery in 1974 when it lost almost a third of its size. Following boundary changes, huge swathes of magnificent countryside were dragged into Oxfordshire.

Oxfordshire can trace a history of settlement going back to the Ice Age. A walk along the ancient Ridgeway reveals remains of ancient settlements from the Neolithic, Bronze and Iron Ages. The Romans, whose influence was so keenly felt in the neighbouring Cotswolds, left considerable evidence of their occupation in this area too. Oxfordshire can claim to be the birthplace of two of England's Kings, Edward the Confessor and Alfred the Great. Oxford became our capital city when the plague decimated London.

Along with much of central England, Oxfordshire did not escape the ravages of the Civil War and Oxford was used as the Royalist headquarters. Banbury was besieged and Radcot, Chalgrove Field, Christmas Common and Cropredy all suffered skirmishes.

The ten tours in this book are linked together in an attempt to form themes and are designed to allow plenty of stops to wander round. We pass temptingly close to some marvellous walking country and a stroll is really the only way to appreciate the many charming towns and villages we visit. The routes use a mixture of main roads and narrow country lanes, where caution must dictate your speed. The directions were correct at the time of writing but please bear in mind that roads are forever being "improved" in the ghastly name of progress.

Space precludes the mention of every attraction in the county; this is not after all a gazetteer. As with my Worcestershire book, I haven't sampled the refreshments in all the places, however tempting a prospect that was! You're all big enough to decide whether you like the look of a pub or teashop menu or not, but I apologise if I've missed your favourite haunt.

The sketch maps (not to scale) will give you an overall idea of the route and arrows indicate the direction of travel. Oxfordshire is annoyingly split over seven OS Landranger maps, (nos 151, 152, 163, 164, 165, 174 and 175), which is hell when you're trying to navigate. However, maps are fascinating companions and will prove invaluable in following sometimes complicated directions. At the end of each Tour under Further Exploration, I've suggested other places, still on the same theme, which you may like to explore in the future. As so many maps are involved, I have also included a map number and grid reference for some of these places. A current telephone number is given so you can verify the opening times of any houses or museums. As with any county full of fascinating places, much has been left unexplored but I hope these tours whet your appetite to wander further afield.

THE AUTHOR

Irene Boston lives in Warwickshire, having spent her early years in London. As a freelance photographer, she supplies images for postcards, calendars, magazines and books. A keen birdwatcher and naturalist, she enjoys walking, local history and exploring as much of Britain as time will allow. Previous walking books have included two on Warwickshire, another on West Midland villages and Secrets of Worcestershire in this same series and a Worcestershire Quiz Book for S.B. Publications.

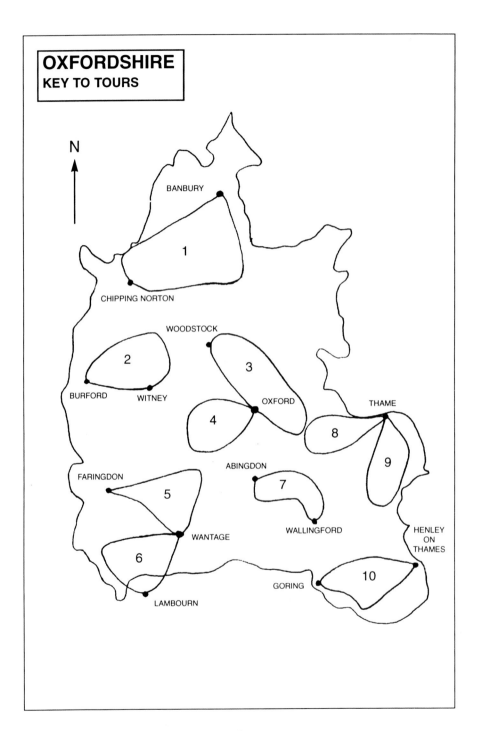

OXFORDSHIRE
KEY TO TOURS

N

BANBURY

1

CHIPPING NORTON

WOODSTOCK

2

BURFORD   WITNEY

3

OXFORD

THAME

4

8

9

ABINGDON

FARINGDON

5

7

WALLINGFORD

HENLEY
ON
THAMES

WANTAGE

6

GORING

10

LAMBOURN

1. MYSTERIOUS OXFORDSHIRE

Over the centuries, the landscape of Britain has changed beyond recognition and a Stone Age man transported to the present day would recognise very little in our countryside. He would also be thoroughly alarmed by our modern technological wonders, but that's another story. In Oxfordshire, prehistoric man left numerous reminders of his existence and many of these finds are now in the county's museums. We also visit more of these fascinating sites on Tour 6.

The mysterious stone circle of the Rollright Stones radiates an extremely powerful, eerie presence. Such atmospheric sites exert a strong hold on the imagination and on a day when, as Shakespeare would say, the "sky doth frown and lour" this place can raise goose bumps on the skin. Theories as to their origin are as numerous as the legends which surround the stones. Part of their appeal lies in the fact that the stones remain completely uncommercialised; thank heavens they don't suffer from the unappealing setting among roads, and a subway, which blight Stonehenge.

Starting from Oxfordshire's northern "capital", Banbury, we see a castle which was a Parliamentary stronghold during the Civil War before we head back several thousand years to the Rollright Stones. Most of the long barrows in this area have vanished under farmland, which makes this surviving stone circle all the more special. Other less well known artefacts in the form of individual stone monoliths and burial chambers are visited. On our return journey we stop at the bustling village of Deddington, once the site of a Norman castle.

TOUR 1
MYSTERIOUS OXFORDSHIRE

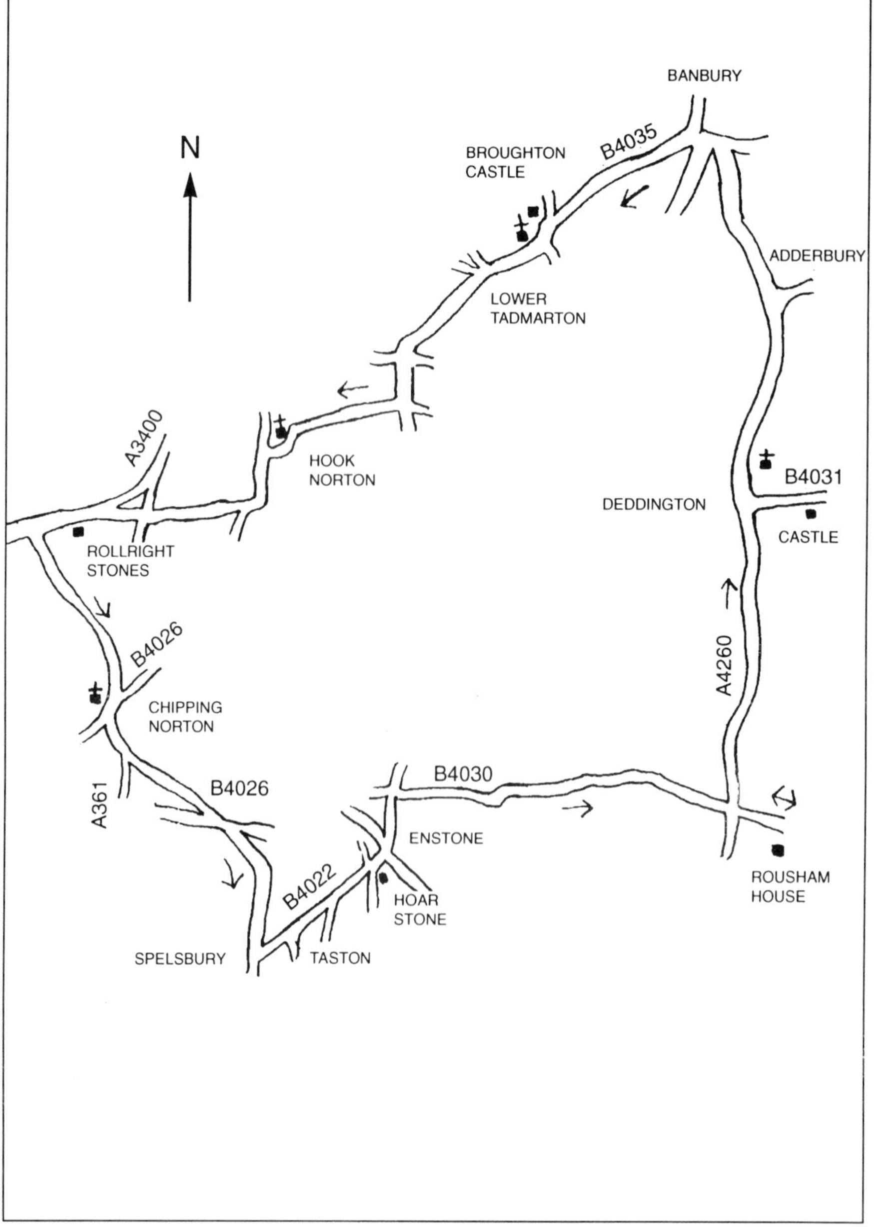

N

BANBURY

BROUGHTON
CASTLE

B4035

ADDERBURY

LOWER
TADMARTON

A3400

HOOK
NORTON

DEDDINGTON

B4031

CASTLE

ROLLRIGHT
STONES

A4260

B4026

CHIPPING
NORTON

A361

B4026

B4030

ENSTONE

B4022

HOAR
STONE

ROUSHAM
HOUSE

SPELSBURY

TASTON

DIRECTIONS: (OS MAPS 151, 164)

From Banbury Cross, join B4035 out to Broughton and turn right in village to Broughton Castle. Return to junction and turn right. At Lower Tadmarton, turn left on minor road, signed Wigginton Heath and go straight over first crossroads. At second crossroads, turn right into Hook Norton.

Continue through village, following signs for Chipping Norton, bearing left and right to Great Rollright. Go straight over crossroads and left on minor road to reach A3400. Turn right and immediately left across A3400 and after 1 mile, reach double layby next to Rollright Stones. At next, almost hidden, crossroads, turn left downhill (change maps!) and turn right through Over Norton. Turn right on B4026 into Chipping Norton.

Follow A361 south, turning left at first roundabout and right at second, signed Burford. Turn left on B4026 to Spelsbury, signed Charlbury. Turn left on minor road, go past turning to Taston and continue to turn left onto B4022. At next crossroads, turn right, signed Fulwell and after 50 yards, park on left. (Hoar Stone hidden in trees at crossroads). Return to junction and turn right. Go straight over staggered crossroads past Enstone and at T-junction, turn right on B4030. Follow B4030 through the Bartons and over A4260 to Rousham House. Return to A4260 and turn right (back on original map), and turn right on B4031 to Deddington. Return to junction and turn right to Banbury.

APPROX DISTANCE: 43 MILES

RECOMMENDED:

Plenty of choice in Banbury and Chipping Norton; Saye & Sele Arms, Tea Rooms, Broughton Castle; The Bell, The Sun, The Pear Tree, Hook Norton; Wyatts Farm Tea Rooms, near Great Rollright; The Box, Carpenters Arms, Middle Barton; Crown & Tuns, Holcombe Hotel, Deddington Arms, Blacksmiths Arms, Unicorn Inn, Horn of Plenty Coffee Shop, Dexters Restaurant, Deddington; Red Lion, Adderbury.

Before you leave BANBURY, take time to explore. The town grew in the shadow of a 12th century castle, although this did not survive beyond the 17th century. Prosaically, a modern shopping centre now stands on the site of the castle. Despite the industrial estates which sprawl ever further into the countryside, Banbury has many things to commend it and a stroll will reveal twisting mediaeval streets, half timbered houses and quaint inns.

In the centre can be found Banbury's most distinctive landmark, the Banbury Cross referred to in the famous nursery rhyme, *"Ride a cock-horse to Banbury Cross, To see a fine lady upon a white horse, With rings on her fingers and bells on her toes, She shall have music wherever she goes"*. It has been suggested that the "fair lady" mentioned may be either Elizabeth I or Celia Fiennes, the 17th century traveller. There have been three crosses scattered through the town in earlier centuries but these were all destroyed by the Puritans. On the present Victorian cross you will find statues of Edward VII, George V and Victoria.

St. Mary's was built in the 1790's to replace the old mediaeval church which was blown up by gunpowder, surely a drastic way of avoiding repair costs. A speciality of the town is the Banbury cake, similar to an Eccles cake, which has been made in Banbury for at least 300 years. Forget the diet, follow your nose to the nearest bakery and treat yourself.

We head west from Banbury to Broughton village, where the fairy tale BROUGHTON CASTLE stands, complete with obligatory moat. The Fiennes family, now the Lords Saye and Sele, have lived here since the mid 15th century and the house is largely unchanged since that time. During the Civil War, secret meetings of leading Parliamentary figures were held here and William Fiennes raised his own regiment which subsequently fought at Edgehill and were known as Lord Saye's Bluecoats. However, William well deserved his nickname of "Old Subtlety" because he managed to turn his own fortunes around and Charles II ended up making him Lord Privy Seal. (Open mid May to mid Sept, Weds, Thurs, Sun - July/August and bank holidays, 2.00-5.00. Admission charge. Tel: 01295 262624).

Mention HOOK NORTON to most people and their eyes will probably light up at the thought of Old Hooky. This traditional ale, which you can find in most local pubs, is still produced by the

Whispering Knights burial chamber, Rollright Stones

brewery on the edge of the village. Although the brewery is not open to the public, there is a shop you can visit. This largely ironstone village occupies a picturesque setting amid rolling countryside. Delightful paths lead down to a stream which crosses a disused railway cutting, now a nature reserve. The massive piers of the viaduct once carried a railway which ran from Banbury to Cheltenham. Dominating the centre of the village is St. Peter's church, topped by an impressive tower which is, in turn, crowned by pinnacles.

We now cross high open country, enjoying superb views as we climb to the ridge bordering Warwickshire, occupied by the ROLLRIGHT STONES. They stand on the ancient Jurassic Way, which ran from the Humber estuary to Salisbury Plain and the coast. Redolent of the past, this remarkable Bronze Age stone circle is known as the King's Men and dates from around 1500BC. Opposite the main circle is the solitary King's Stone and a short walk along the lane is the burial chamber, the Whispering Knights. An intriguing legend claims that the stones are a king and his army. It is claimed that on the summit of the hill, they confronted a witch who prophesised that "If Long Compton thou canst see, King of

Bliss Tweed Mill (now converted to flats), Chipping Norton

England shalt thou be" - a promise the canny witch knew was impossible as the village is hidden from view by a mound. The king and his followers were duly turned to stone and his soldiers form the main circle. The Whispering Knights are alleged to be soldiers who plotted against their sovereign, hence the name of the chamber. Another story alleges that the King's Stone will bleed if pricked at the witching hour of midnight and that the stones cannot be counted. I'll leave that one to you but I've read that there should be around 77 stones. (Although ownership of the site has recently changed hands, it's currently accessible at any reasonable time. The nominal entrance fee is donated to charity).

CHIPPING NORTON, or Chippy as it's affectionately called, is full of character with many elegant buildings. Seventeenth century almshouses stand near St. Mary's, whose size and quality is indicative of Chipping Norton's past prosperity. The church has one of the most impressive naves in the county, with clerestory windows along its entire length creating a wonderfully airy interior. The Decorated east window is believed to have originated in Bruern Abbey, and you can also see Tudor and Stuart glass. In a field beyond the churchyard, bumps and mounds are all that remain of a Norman

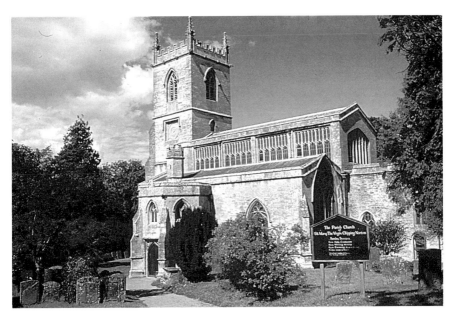

St Mary's Church, Chipping Norton

Almshouses, Chipping Norton

motte and bailey castle. In the valley below, the eye is drawn to the incredible Italianate chimney of the Bliss Tweed Mill, designed by George Woodhouse for William Bliss. Production ceased in 1980 and the building has now been converted into flats. The small theatre, formerly a Salvation Army hostel, is a popular venue and the Museum houses a collection of items from the Bliss Mill, as well as other exhibits of local history. (Open Easter to end Oct, Tues to Sun, 2.00-4.00 plus bank holidays. Admission charge. Tel: 01608 658518).

We pass close by the THOR STONE, which at six feet high and situated in a hedge in the centre of Taston, is named after Thor, the Norse god of thunder. Also in the hamlet is a stunted cross on a minute green. The HOAR STONE, Enstone, near the crossroads, is easily overlooked and consists of a ruinous megalithic tomb of stones standing in a walled enclosure.

We now head east to the unspoilt ROUSHAM HOUSE, originally built in 1635 by Sir Robert Dormer and still owned by the same family. But it is for its magnificent gardens that Rousham is justly famous. You can wander through a landscaped garden filled with

The Hoar Stone (a ruined megalithic tomb), near Enstone

statues, follies, a temple, cascades, a portico and many other ornamental features. They were all designed by William Kent, who was responsible for numerous public buildings in London, including Horse Guards Parade, and the gardens remain much as he left them. (Gardens open daily, all year, 10.00-4.30. House open April to Sept, Weds, Suns and bank holidays, 2.00-4.30. Admission charge. Tel: 01869 347110).

It is recorded in the Domesday Book that DEDDINGTON was an important market town, twice the size of Banbury, with a sizeable "Pudding and Pie" fair held each November. Today, this lively village is still of considerable size with all the bustle of a small town. Although the Norman Castle is signed from the main road, there is no car park - you will have to park in the village centre and walk west through the village. In any case there is very little to see, unless you can get excited by grass ramparts covered in trees. Piers Gaveston, Edward II's notorious favourite who almost cost the King his crown, was held prisoner here by the Earl of Warwick before he was hanged on Blacklow Hill in Warwickshire in 1312. Nearby Castle Farm was built with stone from the castle and Charles I is believed to have slept there before the Battle of Edgehill in 1642, and why not? He seems to have slept everywhere else! The church tower, although impressive, is a shadow of its former glory when the spire was once the tallest in Oxfordshire. In 1635, it collapsed, demolishing much of the church in the process.

FURTHER EXPLORATION:

We visit WITTENHAM CLUMPS on TOUR 7 while WAYLAND'S SMITHY long barrow and UFFINGTON CASTLE are covered on TOUR 6. The whole area of the Downs is riddled with ancient tumuli and evidence of past settlements. Of particular interest is the area around Seven Barrows (map 174, grid ref 327827).

The Iron Age earthwork on BADBURY HILL (map 163, grid ref 262945), near Faringdon, is now under the protection of the National Trust. The wooded hilltop offers tranquil woodland walks and marvellous views.

2. ROMAN REMAINS

As you travel west from Oxford the style of architecture and the whole feel of the countryside undergo a striking change, leading to the inevitable christening of this area as the Oxfordshire Cotswolds. Along the Windrush valley can be found villages, built of the unmistakable Gloucestershire golden stone, which blend perfectly into this rolling landscape. At times it's hard to tell where one county ends and the other begins.

Oxfordshire's proximity to the Fosse Way, that great Roman "motorway" which served as a vital artery linking the Humber to the Severn estuary, ensured extensive settlement by the Romans. Over the years, numerous examples of their occupation have been discovered. Lush river valleys were chosen as sites for villas in both north-west Oxfordshire and the area around Wantage. Romano-British towns grew up in places we now know as Dorchester on Thames and Alchester, near Bicester. Roman legions tramped along another major Roman road, Akeman Street, which crosses Oxfordshire from east to west. In places, this ancient highway is still traversed by modern tarmac roads, most noticeably near Kirtlington, north of Oxford. Public footpaths follow large sections of the route and a study of OS Map 164 will reveal many possibilities for tracing the footsteps of Roman centurions. Roman cemeteries have been discovered at Wheatley and Abingdon. These, together with a bath-house at Headington, indicate the extent to which Roman culture once dominated our kingdom.

This tour will sample only a fragment of this Roman influence. Although most sites have been excavated, very few are open to visitors. In fact you might say that, despite starting from Witney, we can't attempt a blanket coverage of the area!

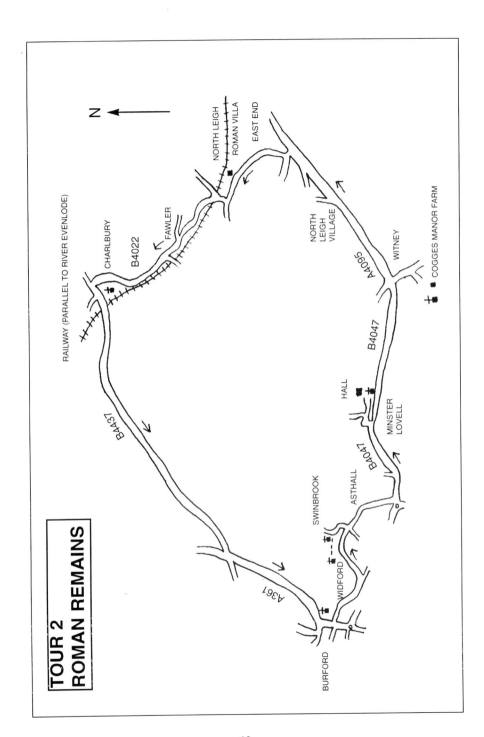

TOUR 2
ROMAN REMAINS

N

RAILWAY (PARALLEL TO RIVER EVENLODE)

CHARLBURY

B4022

FAWLER

NORTH LEIGH
ROMAN VILLA

EAST END

NORTH LEIGH VILLAGE

WITNEY

A4095

COGGES MANOR FARM

B4047

B4437

HALL

MINSTER LOVELL

ASTHALL

B4047

SWINBROOK

WIDFORD

A361

BURFORD

DIRECTIONS: (OS MAPS 163, 164)

Leave Witney on A4095 past North Leigh village and follow brown tourist signs for Roman Villa. Turn left on minor road and shortly, turn right through East End to layby at end of village to park for Roman Villa.

Continue on minor road downhill to crossroads. Turn right, signed Stonesfield, over river Evenlode and immediately after railway bridge, turn left, signed Fawler. At T-junction, turn left through Fawler, ignore left turn and at T-junction, turn right on B4022 to Charlbury. Turn left to reach Charlbury centre.

From Charlbury, join B4437 heading west and signed Burford. Continue on B4437 (change maps) to A361 and turn left into Burford. From almost opposite the cross at top end of Burford High Street, turn left down narrow lane, Swan Lane, and at next crossroads turn left. At T-junction, turn right on minor road which leads through Widford and turn left at crossroads into Swinbrook. Return over bridge in Swinbrook and turn left. Bear right through Asthall to reach B4047. (Back on original map). Turn left and after 2 miles, turn left to follow signs for Minster Lovell Hall. Return to B4047 and turn left to Witney.

APPROX DISTANCE: 30 MILES

RECOMMENDED:

Ample choice in Witney, Charlbury and Burford; Café, Cogges Farm Museum; Leather Bottel, East End; The Swan, Swinbrook; Maytime Inn, Asthall; White Hart, Old Swan, Minster Lovell.

Our journey starts from the bustling town of WITNEY whose name, as you'll have gathered from my earlier appalling pun, is synonymous with blanket making. This traditional industry has exerted a considerable influence on the town and surrounding villages. The closeness to the sheep-rich Cotswolds and the ready availability of water power from the river Windrush were key factors in its development. Famed for their high quality, the blankets were also exported to America. All the blankets made in the area were brought to the Blanket Hall to be weighed, measured and given the seal of approval. An exploration of the surrounding streets reveals many unspoilt gems. Finely proportioned Georgian houses occupy Wood Green. The 17th century Town Hall and the Buttercross, where sheep were bought and sold, can be seen in Market Square.

The awesome proportions of St. Mary's, and the superb spire which soars above the huge tower, make this church a landmark for miles around. There has been a church on this site since Saxon times although only a fragment of the Norman edifice remains.

A step away by the river Windrush is Cogges Manor Farm, a

North Leigh Roman villa

14

museum devoted to showing rural life in Victorian times. The farm is run exactly as it would have been at the turn of the century with not a combine harvester in sight. Staff wear traditional costumes and there are demonstrations of lacemaking, spinning, hurdlemaking, shearing and butter making. Rare breeds, such as Oxford Down sheep and Berkshire pigs, will delight children. (Open March to Nov, Tues to Fri 10.30-5.30, weekends 12.00-5.30. Admission charge. Tel: 01993 772602).

Our next destination is the NORTH LEIGH ROMAN VILLA which confusingly isn't in North Leigh village but on the edge of the hamlet of East End. I suppose East End Roman Villa doesn't have quite the same ring to it. From the layby, follow the footpath downhill to the site which lies near the river and about a mile from the Roman Akeman Street. There is evidence of several Roman villas in this area but this is the only one accessible. Visitors to this English Heritage site can appreciate the layout of the foundations and, through a viewing window, a fine mosaic pavement. The sixty rooms were arranged around three sides of a courtyard with three sets of baths and enjoyed the luxury of underfloor heating. Evidence of settlement can be traced back to the first or second century and by the fourth, the villa was at its most sophisticated, although it had been deserted barely a hundred years later. (Open all year, at any reasonable time. Free admission. Regional Office tel: 01993 881830).

We pass through the hamlet of Fawler, where the remains of a Roman villa with a mosaic floor were unearthed near the river, although these are not visible today. Situated in the Evenlode valley and noted for its history of glove making, CHARLBURY boasts a remarkable array of stone houses. Charlbury Museum is also of interest and contains displays of traditional crafts. (Open Easter to Oct, Suns and bank holidays, 2.00-4.00. Small admission charge. Tel: 01608 810060).

The beautiful town of BURFORD is often claimed by the Cotswolds but it is, just, in Oxfordshire. The steep high street, lined with honey coloured houses, leads down to the river Windrush. Burford is thronged with visitors during the summer and is best appreciated in the early morning or evening when the golden stone glows in the setting sun.

Wealth derived from the wool trade endowed Burford's magnifi-

St John the Baptist Church, Burford

Tolsey Museum, Burford

cent parish church. St. John the Baptist owes its air of nobility and grandeur to the rich merchants who added many aisles and chapels, perhaps in an attempt to ensure a first class ticket to Heaven when their time came. Of particular note are the outstanding tombs both inside and out. During the Civil War, the church was the setting for a violent incident. A group of soldiers took shelter from Cromwell in the church, but even this supposedly inviolate sanctuary couldn't protect them. Several days later, Parliamentary troops entered the church, rounded up and shot the ringleaders. One of their number, Anthony Sedley,

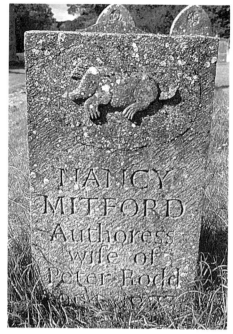

Grave of Nancy Mitford, St Mary's churchyard, Swinbrook

carved his name on the font, adding the word "prisoner".

Of the many charming buildings in Burford, several stand out including the Warwick almshouses, founded in 1457 by Warwick the Kingmaker, Burford Priory, Falkland Hall, the old building of Burford Grammar School and the Tolsey Museum. (Open March to Nov, daily, weekdays 2.00-5.00, weekends and bank holidays 11.00-5.00. Admission charge. Tel: 01367 810294).

Untouched SWINBROOK lies in the lush Windrush valley and the churchyard draws many visitors to the simple grave of the author Nancy Mitford. She lies alongside her sister, Unity and Nancy's grave is marked with the family symbol, a mole. The sisters spent part of their childhood at the manor house in nearby Asthall. Dominating the chancel, and in complete contrast to these unadorned graves, are the extraordinary three-tiered Fettiplace monuments which commemorate six generations of this powerful landowning family. The stone figures all recline rather bizarrely on their right elbows. If you can tear yourself away from this ostentatious display, take a look at the richly carved misericords.

From behind the church, follow a footpath across fields to reach the humble church at WIDFORD, set among water meadows. St. Oswald's is all that remains of a mediaeval village, the bumps and hollows in the ground giving some indication of the layout of the houses and fields which surrounded it. Remarkably, the church was built on the site of a Roman villa and during restorations in 1904, part of a Roman mosaic was found under the chancel floor. The mosaic, which may date from the middle of the 4th century, is now covered to prevent what the church leaflet diplomatically calls "souvenir hunting", but what is clearly attempted theft. Roman objects are still occasionally uncovered during gravedigging and the chief items of interest still to be seen include the 14th century wall paintings and box pews.

We now head for MINSTER LOVELL HALL on the edge of Minster Lovell village. Limited parking is possible outside but a pleasant alternative is to walk through the picturesque thatched cottages in the village to the atmospheric ruins, which stand in meadowland bordering the river Windrush. The ruins are now in the care of English Heritage but were once the home of the Lovell family, including Francis Lovell, a Yorkist and Lord Chamberlain to Richard III. He is perhaps best remembered in the rhyme "The Cat, the Rat and Lovell the Dog, Rule all England under the Hog", which, although not written by Shakespeare, was used by Laurence Olivier in his film of Richard III. The references to the cat and rat refer to Catesby and Ratcliffe, other prominent supporters of Richard, "the hog" of the rhyme referring to the boar on his coat of arms.

Lovell escaped the ruin of Richard's reign at Bosworth Field in 1485 but two years later he supported Lambert Simnel in his ill-fated attempt to claim Henry VII's throne. Fleeing from this battle, he is believed to have returned to Minster Lovell. During altera-tions to the Hall in 1708, a gruesome discovery was made. Behind a wall, a human skeleton was found seated at a table. Legend has it that when Francis returned to the Hall, he hid in a secret room and was provided with food by a servant. When the servant died, Francis inevitably died too - of starvation.

Inhabitants of the Hall seemed to have a fetish for hiding away in secret places. The legend of the Mistletoe Bough tells of a bride who played, of all things, hide and seek on her wedding night. She

Minster Lovell Hall

locked herself in a trunk and was unable to escape. Her skeleton was not found until years later. One wonders what the bridegroom was doing to let his bride go missing - off with the bridesmaids perhaps? (Open all year, at any reasonable time. Free admission. Tel: Regional Office 01179 750700).

FURTHER EXPLORATION:

We visit the old Roman settlements of WALLINGFORD and DORCHESTER ON THAMES on TOUR 7. Nearby, Appleford was once the site of a Romano-British settlement and in 1968, ironware and pewter plates were unearthed. This collection, known as the Appleford Hoard, is now in the Ashmolean Museum in Oxford. South of Bicester, lies the site of Roman Alchester with an old Roman road running close by.

3. ON THE TRAIL OF . . . .

Despite its long history, fascinating architecture and bustling university life, a large number of visitors come to Oxford because of only one thing, or rather, one person - Inspector Morse! The grumpy policeman, played on TV by the marvellous John Thaw, and the long suffering Sergeant Lewis, have found their way into the nation's hearts.

However, the list of distinguished names connected to Oxford is enormous and we can mention barely a fraction of them. For 30 years the Inkling literary group, including C.S. Lewis and J.R.R. Tolkien, met in the Eagle and Child pub in St. Giles, which is also one of Morse's favourite watering holes. Balliol College has produced a number of famous writers and statesmen, including Graham Greene, Gerard Manley Hopkins, Matthew Arnold, Harold Macmillan and Edward Heath. A mathematics don at Christ Church, Reverend C.L. Dodgson (pseudonym Lewis Carroll), wrote *Alice's Adventures in Wonderland* for Alice Liddell, the daughter of the Dean.

Oxford has been used countless times by film and television companies as a backdrop to their productions. *Shadowlands*, the incredibly moving film depicting the true love story of C.S. Lewis and Joy Gresham, was filmed here while television series which have used the city include Evelyn Waugh's *Brideshead Revisited* and John le Carré's *Tinker, Tailor, Soldier, Spy*.

Blenheim Palace has appeared on screen, not only in the Morse story *The Way Through the Woods*, but also in the new film of *Black Beauty* and as the setting for an atmospheric Elsinore in Kenneth Branagh's magnificent version of *Hamlet*.

One practical tip - use the park and ride system. This is far more convenient than struggling through the city's horrendous traffic. Remember, Morse is the only person who can easily find a parking place in Oxford!

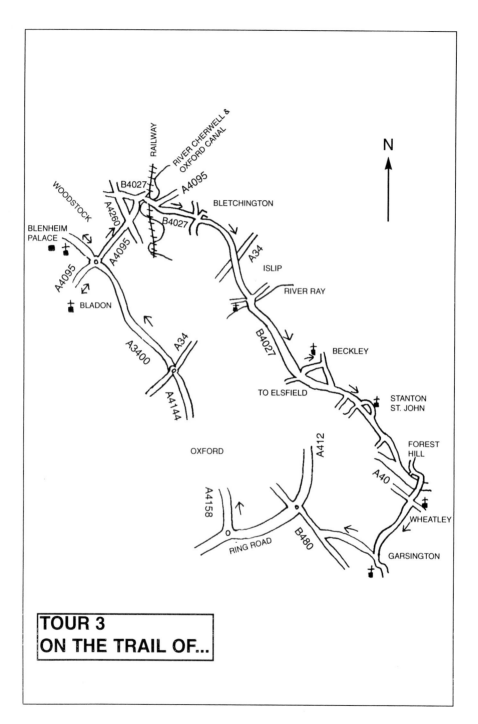

N

RAILWAY

RIVER CHERWELL & OXFORD CANAL

A4095

B4027

WOODSTOCK

A4260

BLETCHINGTON

B4027

BLENHEIM PALACE

A4095

A34

A4095

ISLIP

A4095

RIVER RAY

BLADON

A3400

A34

B4027

BECKLEY

A4144

TO ELSFIELD

STANTON ST. JOHN

OXFORD

A412

FOREST HILL

A40

A4158

WHEATLEY

RING ROAD

B480

GARSINGTON

TOUR 3
ON THE TRAIL OF...

22

DIRECTIONS: (OS MAP 164)

Follow A3400 (still labelled A44 on some maps but as A3400 on road signs!), north from Oxford and turn left at roundabout on A4095 to visit Bladon. Return to A3400 and turn left to Woodstock. Return to roundabout and turn left on A4095, signed Bicester.

Turn left at T-junction with A4260 and almost immediately right on A4095. At T-junction with B4027, turn right to drive over canal and railway. Where road splits, continue ahead on B4027 to Bletchington. Go over A34 to reach Islip. Follow one way system through village and after 3 miles, turn left to Beckley.

Return to B4027, turn left and continue past Stanton St. John and through Forest Hill to briefly join A40. Turn left and within half a mile, turn left, signed Waterperry to a T-junction. Turn right, (road goes over A40) into Wheatley. Follow signs for Garsington, straight over roundabout and the next crossroads and at next junction, go straight over, up Station Road. Follow minor road through Garsington, follow hairpin bend right to reach B480 where a right turn leads back to Oxford.

APPROX DISTANCE: 32 MILES

RECOMMENDED:

Oxford can offer a different place to eat for almost every day of the year; The Royal Swan, A3400; The Lamb, Park House Tea Room, White House, Bladon; Plenty of choice in Woodstock; Restaurant and tea rooms, Blenheim Palace; Rock of Gibraltar, by canal; Black's Head, Bletchington; Swan Inn, Red Lion, Islip; Abingdon Arms, Beckley; Star Inn, Talk House, Stanton St. John; King's Arms, White Horse, Forest Hill; The Railway, Wheatley; The Plough, Red Lion, Garsington.

It's hard to think of a more apt description of OXFORD than Matthew Arnold's phrase "that sweet City with her dreaming spires". Hemmed in by a circle of hills and the rivers Thames and Cherwell, the layout of the city has barely changed in a thousand years. It has one of the most beautiful High Streets in the country, if you can ignore the bumper to bumper traffic. The sheer variety of places to visit is overwhelming, leading to a temptation to rush around like a madman trying to see everything - a panic stricken reaction common to writers who have a tough time deciding what to include and agonising over what to leave out! Buy a town plan, wear good walking shoes and take things slowly.

But first, back to Morse. Many locations in the City and surrounding villages have been used in episodes from the immensely popular series, based on the novels by Colin Dexter. Most of the original books have now been filmed. We must content ourselves with an annual fix in the form of 'specials' as the latest book is filmed, although frequent repeats keep withdrawal symptoms at bay for the millions of Morse addicts like myself.

If you're lucky, you may come across these 'specials' being filmed, easy to spot if they're using that distinctive red Jaguar. Run by the tourist office, Inspector Morse walking tours set off on Mondays, Wednesday and Saturdays between March and October and offer a marvellous opportunity to see the locations used. There are also several other walking tours you can enjoy, covering Oxford past and present, the colleges, the life of William Morris, ghosts and the Civil War. Tickets from the Oxford Information Centre (Tel: 01865 726871).

From the 12th century, Oxford began to emerge as a seat of learning. The traditional "town and gown" rivalries can be traced back to this period and these differences continued through the centuries, particularly in the 17th when the city declared for the Parliamentary forces while the university was mainly Royalist. Charles I held his court at Christ Church during the Civil War and Charles II used Oxford as his temporary capital while the plague swept through London.

To gain an impression of Oxford's history from prehistoric times to the present day, visit The Museum of Oxford in St. Aldates. (Open all year, Tues-Sat 10.00-5.00. Free admission. Tel: 01865 815559). Complementing this is The Oxford Story, which brings to life the sights, sounds and even smells of university life from mediaeval times to the present day. (Open daily, April to Oct 9.30-5.00, July and Aug till 7.00, Nov-March 10.00-4.00. Admission charge. Tel: 01865 790055).

Among the many museums in Oxford, the Ashmolean is one of the most outstanding in the country. Exhibits include Egyptian artefacts, material from excavations in Crete, the Herberden Coin Room, bronzes, paintings, prints, ceramics and Oriental art. (Open all year, Tues-Sat 10.00-4.00, Sun 2.00-4.00, plus bank holidays. Free admission. Tel:01865 278000). Other museums include the Museum of the History of Science (Open all year, Mon to Fri, closed lunchtime. Free admission. Tel:01865 277280) and the Pitt Rivers Museum. (Open all year, Mon to Sat, 1.00-4.30. Free admission. Tel:01865 274726).

The majority of colleges can be visited most afternoons, with some open all day during the university vacations. Check with the Tourist Office for up to date timings. Colleges of particular architectural and historical interest include All Souls', Balliol, Brasenose, Christ Church and Corpus Christi. Some of the finest views of the city can be enjoyed from the top of Carfax Tower. (Open daily April to end Oct, 10.00-5.30 and Nov to end March, 10.00-3.30. Admission charge. Tel: 01865 792653).

If you can tear yourself away, BLADON is our first stop, where St. Martin's church has become a place of pilgrimage. Several generations of the Churchill family are buried in the churchyard, including

Sir Winston himself. His simple white headstone is often decorated with flowers. Following his funeral at St. Paul's Cathedral, his coffin was brought by special train to nearby Hanborough Station and then conveyed to Bladon. Continue to the

Churchill family plot, churchyard,
St Martin's church, Bladon

delightful town of WOODSTOCK, which manages to retain the feel of a village, despite its size and the sheer number of visitors. From the 16th century, glove making was an important local industry and visiting monarchs were always presented with a pair of leather gloves. Of special interest are the elegant buildings, quirky stocks with five holes and the County Museum. (Open all year, Tues to Sat, 10.00-5.00, 4.00 during winter. Sun 2.00-5.00. Admission charge. Tel: 01993 811456).

Bridge and lake, Blenheim Park

For sheer splendour and opulence, few stately homes can match Blenheim Palace. Its Baroque style, designed by Sir John Vanbrugh, is outrageously over the top but endlessly fascinating and the house is now one of the most popular attractions in England, a must on the itinerary of foreign tourists. The seat of the Spencer Churchills, the Dukes of Marlborough, and the birthplace of Sir Winston, it was originally built and paid for by a grateful nation for John Churchill. He was the hero of the Spanish War of Succession and famous for his victory at the Battle of Blenheim in Bavaria in 1704. The site chosen was already a Royal site, a hunting lodge in the ancient manor of Woodstock, and the birthplace of the Black Prince. It was also a favourite refuge for Plantagenet Kings, including Henry II, who installed his mistress, Rosamund Clifford, there. The future Elizabeth I was imprisoned here in 1554 by Mary Tudor.

The magnificent collection of treasures includes tapestries, sculptures, furniture, paintings and an exhibition of Winston's life, as well as 10,000 volumes in the Long Library, enough to keep any bookworm happy for years. In the grounds, you'll find an Italian garden, French water terraces, arboretum, adventure playground,

Rosamund's Well, Blenheim Park

butterfly house, narrow-gauge railway and boat trips. Plenty to keep a family amused for several days. (Open daily, mid March to end Oct, 10.30-5.30. Admission charge. Tel: 01993 811325).

When the bustle of the Palace becomes too much, escape to the Park. Several public footpaths cross Blenheim Park, or you can pay to walk around it all year; useful in the winter when the house is closed. From Fair Rosamund's Well, you can enjoy the classic view of Vanburgh's Bridge.

BLETCHINGTON, with its cluster of fine stone cottages surrounding a leafy village green, occupies a high ridge with views across Otmoor and the Oxford Canal. The 18th century mansion of Bletchington Park stands on the site of a Royalist stronghold which surrendered to Cromwell in 1645.

We move on to ISLIP which stands at the confluence of the rivers Ray and Cherwell, always a crossing of strategic importance. The peaceful air of the village belies its violent past. During the Civil War, Cromwell watched from the church tower as his troops overcame the Queen's Regiment at the Battle of Islip Bridge in 1645. Edward the Confessor was born at a royal palace here in 1003 and in his will, he gave the manor to the Abbey he had founded at Westminster. His full length portrait and the words of the King's charter can be seen in St. Nicholas church.

Slightly off our route lies ELSFIELD, where John Buchan and R.D. Blakemore once made their homes. Our road climbs towards the picturesque cottages of BECKLEY, known as one of the Seven Towns of Otmoor. Evelyn Waugh lived at the Abingdon Arms for a time. Inside St. Mary's can be seen remnants of magnificent wall paintings depicting the Last Judgement. We pass close by STANTON ST. JOHN, the birthplace of John White, one of the founders of the state of Massachusetts. In the 17th century, the poet, John Milton, was married at the church in Forest Hill to a local girl.

Portrait of Edward the Confessor, St Nicholas Church, Islip

Ever under threat from the expansion of Oxford, GARSINGTON clings to its village identity. The manor house was once the home of Lady Ottoline Morrell, the renowned hostess who entertained numerous writers and artists. Her list of famous guests includes T.S. Eliot, H. Rider Haggard, Aldous Huxley, Bertrand Russell, Virginia Woolf, D.H. Lawrence, Maynard Keynes and Siegfried Sassoon.

FURTHER EXPLORATION:

There are far too many famous names, both real and fictional, to mention here but we do visit SUTTON COURTENAY on TOUR 7, the burial place of George Orwell and former Prime Minister Asquith. On TOUR 6 we pass close to the village of UFFINGTON, the home of Sir John Betjeman for some years. You can also visit Tom Brown's Schooldays Museum which illustrates the life and works of the author, Thomas Hughes, who was born in the village. (Open Easter to Oct, weekends and bank holidays except Aug BH, 2.00-5.00. Small admission charge. Tel: 01367 820259).

4. A LIVING RIVER BY THE DOOR
(Robert Louis Stevenson)

For centuries, the Thames was one of the principal trade routes in southern England and the opening of canals like the Oxford, Thames and Severn, and the Kennet and Avon significantly increased its importance. However, the arrival of the railway and later, the road network contributed to the decline in trade and now the majority of river craft are leisure boats. The Thames, whose Celtic name means "dark water", rises humbly in a field near Cirencester and meanders across Gloucestershire into Oxfordshire. Constantly fed by tributaries, the river increases speed and width on its journey to the Thames estuary, a distance of some 180 miles. Running through a tranquil landscape, the river itself, although fast flowing and powerful, is a gentle giant with no dramatic gorges or cataracts.

The tributaries of the upper Thames were once famed for their salmon. However, by the 19th century, the river had become virtually an open sewer and it's really only in modern times that efforts to clean it up have been successful. During the 19th century, in an attempt to control the power of the river, and reduce regular and disastrous flooding, a system of locks, cuts, weirs and sluices was constructed.

Towards the end of the 1800's, messing about in boats became a favourite pastime, fuelled by the popularity of Jerome K. Jerome's book, *Three Men in a Boat*. There are few more peaceful ways of travelling than by boat. After all, who would argue with Ratty in *Wind in the Willows* when he was asked, "And you really live by the River? What a jolly life!", to which he replied "By it and with it or on it and in it, It's my world, and I don't want any other".

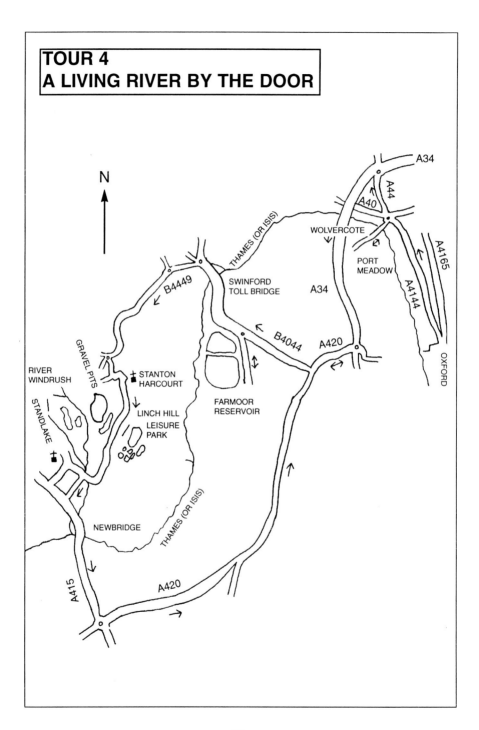

TOUR 4
A LIVING RIVER BY THE DOOR

N

A34

A44

A40

WOLVERCOTE

A4165

THAMES (OR ISIS)

SWINFORD
TOLL BRIDGE

A34

PORT
MEADOW

B4449

B4044

A420

A4144

OXFORD

GRAVEL PITS

RIVER
WINDRUSH

STANTON
HARCOURT

FARMOOR
RESERVOIR

STANDLAKE

LINCH HILL
LEISURE
PARK

NEWBRIDGE

THAMES (OR ISIS)

A415

A420

DIRECTIONS: (OS MAP 164)

Head north along A4144 from Oxford and turn left at roundabout through Wolvercote to visit Port Meadow, car park at grid ref 486094. Return to roundabout and turn left, along A44 and at next roundabout turn left onto A34. Leave at next junction, and turn right on A420. Within one mile, turn left onto B4044 and at T-junction, turn right, signed Farmoor. At roundabout, turn left to reach Farmoor Reservoir.

Return to roundabout and turn left, still on B4044. Cross Swinford toll bridge (5p toll, queues possible) and at roundabout turn left, on B4449. Keep left at next roundabout and after 3 miles, turn left at roundabout into Stanton Harcourt. Continue on minor road through village and past Linch Hill Leisure Park. On reaching Standlake, take first left, signed Bampton to reach A415. Turn left over Newbridge to roundabout. Turn left and follow A420 back to Oxford.

APPROX DISTANCE: 28 MILES

RECOMMENDED: The Trout Inn, Wolvercote; The Talbot, Swinford; The Fox, Harcourt Arms, Stanton Harcourt; Cafe, Linch Hill Leisure Park; The Bell, Black Horse, Standlake; Rose Revived, Newbridge.

We soon escape from the bustle of Oxford to PORT MEADOW, sandwiched between the Oxford Canal and the Thames, or, as it's still known here in the city, the Isis. The Thames valley is a vital landmark for thousands of migrating birds who follow this great gash in the landscape as they fly between the Thames and Severn estuaries. Of equal importance is the abundant bird life the river supports. The mute swan is the most obvious symbol of the river, and these majestic birds are slowly recovering their numbers following the banning of lead weights in fishing.

Port Meadow has never seen pesticides or the plough and remains a valuable habitat for many birds where grazing cattle and horses enrich the abundant flora. During winter, the meadow floods regularly and the shallow pools created attract huge numbers of wigeon, teal and shoveler, as well as lapwing, Canada geese and swans. For birdwatchers, an early morning visit is recommended, particularly during the summer when the sheer numbers of visitors later in the day create considerable disturbance for the birds.

Our next watery stop is at FARMOOR RESERVOIR, where activities such as windsurfing, angling and sailing are enjoyed by many visitors. On the western edge of Farmoor, Pinkhill Meadow Nature Reserve has been created jointly by Thames Water and the National Rivers Authority. The wet meadows, reed pools, scrub and muddy scrapes are specifically designed to attract a wider variety

River Thames by Godstow Nunnery, Port Meadow, near Oxford

Farmoor Reservoir

of species than the reservoir alone can support. A superb walk circles the reservoir, skirting Pinkhill Meadow and this whole area, (if you'll pardon the pun), offers far more(!) than you would realise at first glance. As most birds will be quite distant across the water, binoculars and preferably a telescope are essential to identify the various species. Permits for birdwatching are available from the gatehouse.

At first glance, the concrete embankments of Farmoor appear rather sterile, with little vegetation or muddy shores so essential to wading birds. It is amazing therefore to discover that many waders make regular stopovers here during the spring and autumn migration. Frequent visitors have included whimbrel, greenshank, sanderling and knot, together with a good scattering of rare species.

During the winter, Farmoor provides a safe haven for ducks such as goldeneye, tufted, pochard, wigeon and the ubiquitous mallard. Because of its sheer size, Farmoor is generally one of the last stretches of water to become ice-bound and is a magnet for any birds in the area. Careful scanning of the massed flocks at such a time may reveal the presence of rarer birds such as scaup, smew, long-tailed duck, common and velvet scoter, as well as unusual grebes. Terns pass through during migration, while some common terns rear their young on the rafts provided. One of Farmoor's major spectacles is the huge gull roost. A couple of hours before dark, gulls will start arriving from their feeding grounds in nearby fields and by the time dusk falls, there could be as many as 10,000 gulls on the water. Reaching a peak in August and September, vast numbers of swifts, swallows, and martins use the reservoir as a service station to replenish food reserves and as many as 15,000 can be seen hawking for insects over the water. It's quite a thrill to stand on the causeway while these agile, elegant birds swoop and dive around you, coming really close but never colliding either with you or each other.

Following a storm, a visit to Farmoor can be very worthwhile. During periods of bad weather, many sea birds become caught up in the weather systems. When they emerge from the cloud and rain, they seek the nearest stretch of water to rest and feed before heading back to their natural habitat, the sea. Many pelagic species, such as gannets, shearwaters, kittiwakes and skuas have been recorded here and the sight of one of these maritime species, way off course, is an amazing thrill. And who knows, if you're really lucky, an osprey may appear overhead.

We move on to cross the Swinford tollbridge over the Thames. Built in the 18th century by the 4th Earl of Abingdon, it is one of only

Abbot's Kitchen and Pope's Tower from St Michael's church, Stanton Harcourt

two remaining bridges which levy a charge. The quaint village of STANTON HARCOURT feels locked in a time capsule. The manor house was built between 1380 and 1470 and the Great Kitchen and Pope's Tower are the only survivors from the original structure. Pope's Tower is so called because Alexander Pope worked for two years on his translation of Homer's Iliad in these rooms. The Great Kitchen is a remarkable structure, reminiscent of the Abbot's Kitchen at Glastonbury Abbey. (Open April to Sept, alternate Thurs and bank holidays, 2.00-6.00. Admission charge. Tel: 01865 881928).

St Edburg's shrine, St Michael's church, Stanton Harcourt

The chief glory of St. Michael's church lies in its elaborate monuments to the Harcourt family, which are in striking contrast to the plain walls of the church. One particularly splendid memorial is to Robert, who was Henry VII's standard bearer at his victory on Bosworth Field, which began the line of Tudor kings. The tattered remnants of the flag hang above the tomb and are a tangible and moving reminder of this fascinating period in history. Fragments of paintings in the chancel and around the window arches are a reminder of how colourful mediaeval churches once were. Near the altar is an ornate canopy

St Michael's church, Stanton Harcourt

from the late 13th century shrine of St. Edburg, which originally supported a chest containing relics of the saint. The canopy was saved from Bicester Priory at the time of the Dissolution. A memorial plaque on the outside of the north wall, with an epitaph by Alexander Pope, records the deaths of John Hewet and Sarah Drew, who were otherwise occupied in a hayfield and failed to notice the approach of a storm. They were both killed by lightning.

The unspoilt river Windrush begins its gentle 30 mile journey from Cutsdean, near Stow on the Wold. At Witney, the Windrush divides into two streams which flow through the STANDLAKE GRAVEL PITS, before rejoining and entering the Thames at Newbridge. Continuing gravel extraction means there is a variety of shallow scrapes and deep pits with well established vegetation. Vicarage Pit is now a nature reserve, managed by the local Wildlife Trust. Other pits form part of the Linch Hill Leisure Park (Tel: 01865 882215) and are used for fishing, sailing, water skiing and windsurfing. Several caravan and camping sites testify to this area's popularity with holiday makers and various public footpaths cross the area, offering good views over many of the pits.

FURTHER EXPLORATION:

On TOUR 7 we pass close by Day's Lock near Little Wittenham which hosts the annual Pooh Sticks World Championships. The river EVENLODE rises in the Cotswolds and meanders through a lush valley to join the Thames to the west of Oxford.

The OXFORD CANAL, completed in 1790, was the first canal to link London with the industrial Midlands via the Thames. The towpath is in excellent condition, offering many miles of enjoyable walking. The Canal and RIVER CHERWELL run parallel for 23 miles, sometimes so closely that during floods one is indistinguishable from the other.

5. A HISTORY IN ALL MEN'S LIVES
(Shakespeare's Henry IV Part II)

Wherever you travel in Britain, a tangible sense of the past surrounds you. Every field, hill and village could tell a story and Oxfordshire, along with much of the Midlands, was involved in many power struggles. On our tour, the Saxons left the greatest impression. Wantage was the birthplace of Alfred the Great, whose defeat of the Danes has passed into legend. When you consider the names of the invaders, it's a blessed relief that Alfred was victorious. Would you want a King called Halfdane or Ivar the Boneless, or their father, Ragnar Leatherbreeches? Names to conjure with! Alfred's establishment of the Kingdom of Wessex is generally regarded as being the foundation of our English nation. He was given the title "The Great", not in recognition of his baking skills, but for his valour, wisdom and civilising influence. At Faringdon, this famous sovereign built a royal palace and his son, Edward the Elder was buried. We also visit a village which has connections with a key figure in the Wars of the Roses.

Oxfordshire was inevitably caught up in the struggles of the Civil War. Oxford became the Royalist headquarters and Faringdon was besieged by Cromwell's troops. Nearby, Radcot is the site of the oldest bridge over the Thames and this crossing was of vital importance in that conflict. Centuries earlier, Radcot had seen a skirmish between Richard II's soldiers and rebels rising up against the power of the monarch. In Further Exploration, we catch up with two Royal mysteries, full of drama and intrigue. One from the Elizabethan era and the other concerns the first of the Plantagenets, Henry II.

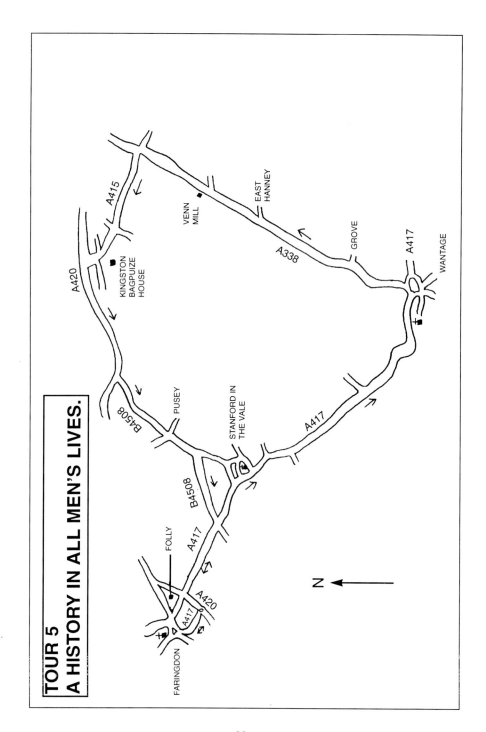

TOUR 5
A HISTORY IN ALL MEN'S LIVES.

FARINGDON
FOLLY
A417
A420
A417
B4508
A417
STANFORD IN THE VALE
PUSEY
B4508
A420
KINGSTON BAGPUIZE HOUSE
A415
VENN MILL
EAST HANNEY
A338
GROVE
A417
WANTAGE

N ←

38

DIRECTIONS: (OS MAPS 163, 164, 174)

Leave Faringdon on A417, turn left on A420 (change maps, 164), and right on A417 and after 3 miles, turn left to Stanford in the Vale. Return to A417 and continue to Wantage, (onto map 174).

Join A338 from Wantage through Grove (back on map 164), and East Hanney past Venn Mill. Turn left on A415 to pass Kingston Bagpuize House and go left on A420. Turn left on B4508 past Pusey House and through Hatford. Turn right on A417 and left on A420 and right again on A417 to return to Faringdon (back onto original map, 163).

APPROX DISTANCE: 28 MILES

RECOMMENDED:

Plenty of choice in Faringdon and Wantage; The Anchor, Stanford in the Vale; Leather Bottle, A417; Coach & Horses, East Challow; The Volunteer, Grove; The Ark, A338; Tea shop, Kingston Bagpuize House.

Our natural starting point is the bustling, market town of FARINGDON, which overlooks the Thames valley and Wessex Downs. The Cotswold wool trade contributed greatly to the town's prosperity which reached its peak in the 15th and 16th centuries. Robert, Earl of Gloucester, built a castle here in 1145 and a charter for a weekly market was granted by King John. During the Civil War siege by Parliamentary forces, Faringdon House, held by the Royalist Sir Robert Pye, was attacked by his own son, a Parliamentarian.

Norman north door, All Saints, Faringdon

Despite its size and modern buildings, Faringdon retains a pleasant atmosphere, enhanced by the attractive market place with its cluster of Georgian fronted shops and popular pubs. Inside the south door of All Saints, decorated by marvellous wrought iron work, lies an interior of great interest which includes a splendid modern concert organ. Have a look at the pillar on the right as you enter. The stone carving on the base, different from the other pillars, is thought to be a tortoise. In the Unton and Pye chapels there is a rich feast of decorated stone work with superb

Folly, Faringdon

memorials. The kneeling figure of Dorothy Unton, hands clasped in prayer, is a fine example of craftsmanship. The lack of a spire can be blamed on the inaccuracy of the soldiers manning Cromwell's battery. These stalwarts destroyed the spire while aiming at Faringdon House behind it. Outside, the north door is a magnificent example of Norman workmanship.

A 100 foot high folly, a distinctive landmark to the east of the town which attracts many visitors, was built in 1935 by Lord Berner on the site of a mediaeval

King Alfred's Statue, Wantage

castle and the Cromwellian battery. It was immediately christened, obviously by people who knew Lord Berner intimately, his "monstrous erection". Apparently, an even sillier sign once hung on the tower, proclaiming that "members of the public committing suicide from this tower do so at their own risk"! (Open April to Oct, first Sunday of each month, 2.00 - 5.00).

We continue to STANFORD IN THE VALE, a large village of exceptional charm which was, until the 16th century, an important market centre. The south porch of St. Denys church was built to celebrate the marriage of Anne Neville, the daughter of Warwick the "Kingmaker", to the Duke of Gloucester, later, of course, Richard III. In the chancel is a piscina which once housed a famous and

King Alfred's School, Wantage

rather gruesome relic from Abingdon Abbey, the finger of St. Denys himself. It's unclear what happened to the rest of him.

Our halfway point is the ancient market town of WANTAGE which owes its existence to the proximity of the Ridgeway. During Roman times, a settlement was established near an abundant water supply and at the meeting place of two roads. As mentioned earlier, Wantage can claim the singular distinction of being the birthplace of an Anglo-Saxon King. Alfred the Great was born here in 849 AD. His statue, clutching a battleaxe in one hand and a manuscript in the other, with not a cake to be seen, can be found in the market place. The effigy, which is surrounded by a bustling market twice a week, is a smaller version of the famous statue at Winchester and was presented to Wantage in 1877.

In 1216, Henry III granted the town a market charter, later confirmed by Edward I. During the industrial revolution, the town became known as "Black Wantage". The decline of traditional trades brought great poverty to the town. Unruly workmen, when not engaged in constructing the Wiltshire and Berkshire canal, roamed the streets; drunkenness and violent fights were common. In 1828, in a desperate attempt to clean up the town, the "Town Improvement Act" was passed. Twenty years later, the Reverend Butler established the largest order of nuns in the Church of England and raised money to restore many ecclesiastical buildings.

Robert Lloyd Lindsay, later Baron Wantage of Lockinge, was a generous benefactor to the town. paying for King Alfred's statue and the new Town Hall. Eagles Close almshouses are a legacy of Thomas Eagle and were provided "as an asylum for decayed housekeepers" - something every town could do with. I think I'll reserve my place now!

St. Peter and St. Paul's church, restored by the famous Victorian architect George Edmund Street, boasts mediaeval choir stalls with intricately carved misericords. One of the first Knights of the Garter, Sir William Fitzwarin, is buried in the church and his badge of office is worn on the leg of the figure on his tomb. In 1849, to commemorate the millenium of King Alfred's birth, a school was built on the Portway.

The Vale and Downland Museum and Visitor Centre, opposite the church, houses displays on the area's history and downland life, as well as an art gallery, crafts shop, coffee shop and tourist information centre. (Open Tues to Sat, 10.30-4.30, Sun 2.30-5.00. Free admission. Tel:01235 760176).

We head north from Wantage, passing VENN MILL, a restored water-powered corn mill standing on a tributary of the river Ock. Wholemeal flour is on sale in a building which dates from around 1800. (Open second Sun in month, April to Oct, 10.00-5.00. Admission charge. Tel: 01367 718888).

Our return route passes close by KINGSTON BAGPUIZE HOUSE, built during the reign of Charles II. The unusual name evolved from the Norman lord of the manor Ralf de Bachepuise. The house can be justly proud of its fine plasterwork and panelling, as well as a superb cantilevered staircase. Scattered among the gardens are a Georgian gazebo built over an Elizabethan cockpit, as well as 17th century stable buildings. (Open Easter to end Sept 2.30-5.30 on selected days - call for details. Admission charge. Tel: 01865 820259).

FURTHER EXPLORATION:

CUMNOR, south west of Oxford, was once the home of Robert Dudley, Earl of Leicester who was Elizabeth I's favourite. Cumnor Place was the scene of a tragedy which has caused endless speculation. Dudley's wife, Amy, was found dead at the bottom of the stairs. A tragic accident or, if she suspected Robert of having an affair with Elizabeth, perhaps suicide. Or, more sinisterly, murder, leaving him free to marry the Queen. Whatever the truth of the matter, as everyone knows, Elizabeth never married.

All that remains of the 12th century GODSTOW NUNNERY in Port Meadow (visited on TOUR 4), is a wall and the ruins of a chapel. Henry II's mistress, Rosamund Clifford, is believed to have retired to Godstow Nunnery. Another legend claims she was murdered by Eleanor, Henry's Queen. Whichever story is correct, she was certainly buried here. Following the Reformation, the nunnery became a private house which later did not survive the Civil War.

We visited ISLIP, birthplace of Edward the Confessor, on TOUR 3 and we'll be exploring WALLINGFORD, the site of a royal castle in TOUR 7.

6. HORSES - ANCIENT AND MODERN

The North Wessex Downs and the Vale of the White Horse are extraordinarily rich in archaeological sites. The hills rise steeply to over 700 feet, forming an escarpment while the plateau which lies beyond is cut into by dry valleys. Our ancestors left evidence of past settlements in the form of burial mounds, ancient fortifications and carved figures. The Uffington White Horse is probably the oldest carved, chalk figure of a horse in Britain. One can only speculate as to the importance this massive chalk symbol played in the lives of local people.

The Ridgeway crosses this wild, lonely countryside and offers superb walking, its broad track running along the top of the chalk downland, where the clarity of the views and the air is invigorating. This track, which partly follows the Icknield Way, has always been a vitally important artery and is one of the oldest highways in Britain. The Ridgeway provided an easier passage for people than the thickly wooded valley floors. Now, a long distance footpath, accorded the status of a National Trail, follows its course from Overton Hill, near Avebury in Wiltshire to Ivinghoe Beacon in Buckinghamshire, or vice versa, depending on which way you travel.

To make this Tour circular, I have taken liberties with the county boundary, straying briefly into Berkshire when we visit Lambourn. A quick look at the map will reveal Lambourn's position in the centre of racehorse country, surrounded by some of the finest stables in the region. The Downs serve as racehorse training grounds and if you're an early riser, you may see the first string of horses being exercised on the gallops.

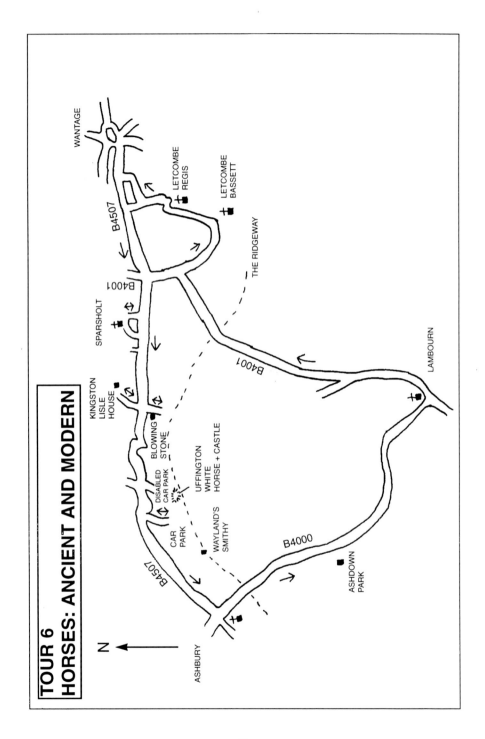

TOUR 6
HORSES: ANCIENT AND MODERN

N

WANTAGE

B4507

LETCOMBE REGIS

LETCOMBE BASSETT

THE RIDGEWAY

B4001

SPARSHOLT

LAMBOURN

B4001

KINGSTON LISLE HOUSE

BLOWING STONE

UFFINGTON WHITE HORSE + CASTLE

DISABLED CAR PARK

CAR PARK

WAYLAND'S SMITHY

B4000

ASHDOWN PARK

B4507

ASHBURY

46

DIRECTIONS: (OS MAP 174)

Leave Wantage on B4507 signed Ashbury, heading west. Go straight over crossroads with B4001, passing minor roads for Sparsholt and Kingston Lisle House. Turn left on second minor road to parking for Uffington White Horse. (First left turning is for disabled parking).

Return to B4507 and turn left to Ashbury. Turn left on B4000 past Ashdown Park and into Lambourn.

Turn left on B4001 across downs and after 6 miles, turn right on minor road to Letcombe Bassett and Regis. Continue through both villages to rejoin B4507 and turn right to Wantage.

APPROX DISTANCE: 26 MILES

RECOMMENDED:

Ample choice in Wantage and Lambourn; The Star Inn, Sparsholt; Blowing Stone Inn, Kingston Lisle; Rose & Crown, Ashbury; The Greyhound, Letcombe Regis.

We start our journey from WANTAGE, visited previously on TOUR 5, where a visit to the Vale and Downland Museum will get you in the mood. We head west passing a turning for unspoilt SPARSHOLT, which is worth a quick detour. The church of the Holy Rood dominates this tiny village and contains three wooden effigies of the Archard family. The Puritans destroyed many such relics and, even if they didn't, any timber effigies rarely survived woodworm. In the Decorated chancel is a nine men's morris, a mediaeval version of draughts which Shakespeare mentions in *Midsummer Night's Dream.*

Also slightly off our route is KINGSTON LISLE HOUSE which is noted for its fine collection of glass, carpets, furniture and a curious staircase, as well as letters written by the Commander-in-Chief in the Crimean War, Lord Raglan. (Open on selected days only, admission fee to charity. Tel:01367 820599). As we rejoin the B4507, a short distance up the road opposite is the Blowing Stone. This was, allegedly, used as a trumpet by King Alfred to summon his army and, in the 18th century, was moved to its present position from White Horse Hill.

We now head up onto the Downs to visit the UFFINGTON WHITE HORSE which has been mentioned in countless books and poems, including Thomas Hughes' *The Scouring of the White Horse,* and G.K. Chesterton's *Ballad of the White Horse.* An 11th century document from Abingdon Abbey is perhaps the first written refer-

The Ridgeway by Uffington Castle

ence to the carved figure, although its exact origins are obscure. One story tells that it was carved to commemorate Alfred's victory over the Danes, another that it was created over 2,000 years ago by Iron Age Celts in honour of Epona, their goddess and protectress of horses. Or that it was the work of the Atrebates, a Belgic tribe in the first century. Whatever the true history, by the 14th century, the horse rivalled Stonehenge as a major tourist attraction. At 365 feet long and 130 feet high, it dominates from many parts

Uffington White Horse

of the Vale but, unless you happen to have a plane handy, it is best seen from a distance. Below the horse is a dry valley called the Manger, where the White Horse is said to feed at night. A more prosaic explanation is that it was formed by melting snow fields during the last Ice Age.

A step away is the ancient hill fort of UFFINGTON CASTLE, which enjoys an equally splendid panorama. The impressive enclosure, formed by grassed ramparts and a ditch, was occupied by downland farmers around 2,500 years ago. During excavations in 1850, an Iron Age coin was found which possibly links the site with the Dobunni tribe. In this area full of legends and stories, one of the most appealing is that of St. George. He is supposed to have slain the famous dragon on the appropriately named Dragon Hill, a flat-topped mound at the foot of the slope. The bare patch is said to be where the dragon's blood was spilt, poisoning the earth.

There is much of interest in this area for the naturalist. The north facing escarpment seems to act as a landmark for migrating birds, a sort of avian highway with service stations scattered along the route! Vast arable fields are bounded by hedgerows, scrub and patches of woodland. In some parts, these precious remnants of cover are so widely scattered as to have the effect of concentrating any birds into a comparatively small area. If you were one of our feathered friends, faced with a prairie desert offering little cover and saturated by pesticides or a berry rich hedgerow offering food and shelter, which would you choose? A day of low cloud and mist following a clear night can be very productive and at such times, the hedges may be alive with birds. Areas of permanent grassland, in use as training gallops, provide additional feeding grounds for the increasingly scarce grey and red-legged partridges.

The remaining unimproved chalk downland supports many endangered species of plant life and insects, particularly butterflies. In such a well drained area, with very few ponds or streams, any area of standing water, even a large puddle, will act as a magnet for all manner of wildlife.

An exhilarating walk west along the Ridgeway for about a mile leads to WAYLAND'S SMITHY neolithic long barrow. Flanked by sarsen stones and surrounded by beech trees, this ancient and eerie burial chamber is thought to date from around 5,000 years ago. The name derives from the Germanic legend about a magical blacksmith called Wayland. Arrive here on horseback and you might care to test another legend. If your horse loses a shoe, leave a silver

Wayland's Smithy Long Barrow, The Ridgeway

penny, plus the horse, at the Smithy and return later to find the horse newly shod, and your money gone. This quirky story dates from the 10th century, so I'm not quite sure what the current charge might be, after allowing for inflation (but don't complain to me if it doesn't work!).

We continue our Tour to ASHBURY village, whose blend of thatched cottages, ancient manor house, church and quaint inn paint an exquisite picture. We now head south to the National Trust property of ASHDOWN HOUSE, nestling deep in the Downs. It was described by Pevsner as the "perfect doll's house" and is believed to have been built for Elizabeth of

Wayland's Smithy Long Barrow, The Ridgeway

Bohemia, Charles I's sister and known as the Winter Queen. However, she died before she could enjoy living there. (Open April to end Oct, Weds and Sat, 2.00-6.00. Closed Easter and bank holidays. Admission charge. Woodland accessible all year, Sat to Thurs. Tel: 01488 72584 or 01904 528051).

On the hill above the house is an Iron Age fort called Alfred's Castle but it's unclear what his connection with the site may have been, as the original fortification predates his reign. We continue across the county border into Berkshire, reaching the lively town of LAMBOURN, where the principal occupation is the breeding and training of racehorses. Scattered around the Downs are stables and signs alongside the surrounding narrow roads warn of the close proximity of the gallops. The return route climbs high onto the downs with glorious far reaching views. Car parks along the way offer the chance to stretch the legs and enjoy more walking along the Ridgeway.

LETCOMBE BASSETT, a picturesque jumble of thatched houses, shelters a humble church which looks much as it did several

Stream, Letcombe Bassett

hundred years ago. Horses trained here have three times won the Grand National. Readers of Thomas Hardy will probably already know that the village inspired Cresscombe in his novel *Jude the Obscure.* We follow a narrow road across the brook, where the watercress beds were once the focus of a thriving industry, into LETCOMBE REGIS. Modern houses jostle with thatched cottages and stone dwellings. In the churchyard of St. Andrew's, is the grave of a Maori chieftain, George King Hirango, who came to this country to train as a minister and died of TB in 1871 at the tragically early age of 19.

FURTHER EXPLORATION:

The Downs are criss-crossed with a multitude of footpaths and if you equip yourself with an OS map, boots, rucksack (and food!), there are endless possibilities for some magnificent walking. Here are just a couple of suggestions: from Blewbury village, walk to the fort on BLEWBURTON HILL (map 174, 547862). A narrow lane leads from East Hendred onto EAST HENDRED DOWN (map 174, 459851), where you can follow the Ridgeway east or west as the fancy takes you.

7. ARCHITECTURAL GEMS

Oxfordshire doesn't have a single unifying style of architecture and you are as likely to encounter limestone, flint or marl as you are thatch and Cotswold stone. On a journey through the county you'll travel from the silvery blue bricks of the Henley and Watlington areas, to the golden stone of the Cotswolds in the west. Along the way, there are thatched cottages nestling under the Wessex Downs, mellow brick houses in the Chiltern villages, while in the north around Banbury the predominant colour derives from the local ironstone.

However, many villages, especially those bordering large towns, have been blighted by "in-fill" housing, not necessarily in a style appropriate to the rest of the village. In villages which have been bypassed, these modern estates often occupy former green fields between the older heart of the village and the new road.

On this Tour we have the opportunity to savour architecture from almost every period, and as diverse and interesting as anywhere in the country. We see ancient cruck cottages, thatched dwellings, elegant brick houses and impressive town buildings. Even the seemingly soulless modern town centres can hold a few surprises. Whatever may occupy the ground floors of shops and offices, the upper storeys often retain a hint of their former glory and character. It is the history behind these buildings and of the people who lived there which is really fascinating. We travel from the ancient abbey at Abingdon, past the hillfort on the Sinodun Hills to the castle at Wallingford and the beautiful buildings of Dorchester, all interspersed with some of the finest countryside in the Thames valley.

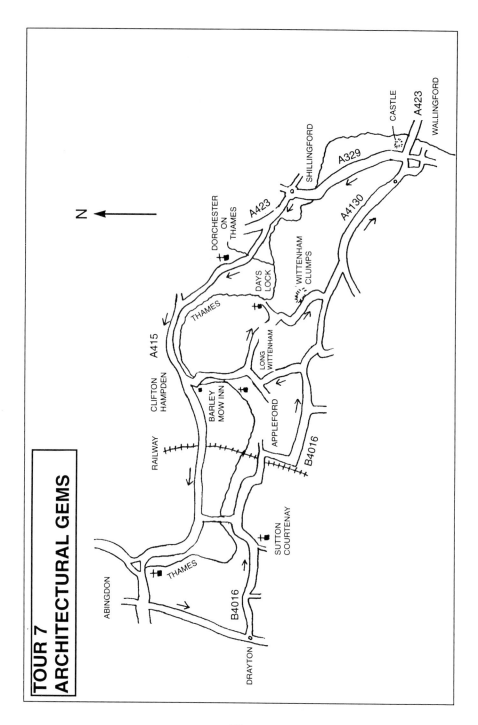

TOUR 7
ARCHITECTURAL GEMS

N ←

DORCHESTER
ON
THAMES

SHILLINGFORD

CASTLE

A423

WALLINGFORD

A423

A329

A4130

DAYS
LOCK

WITTENHAM
CLUMPS

THAMES

A415

LONG
WITTENHAM

CLIFTON
HAMPDEN

BARLEY
MOW INN

APPLEFORD

RAILWAY

B4016

SUTTON
COURTENAY

ABINGDON

THAMES

B4016

DRAYTON

DIRECTIONS: (OS MAPS 164, 175)

Leave Abingdon on B4017, south to Drayton. Turn left at rounda-bout onto B4016 to Sutton Courtenay. Continue on B4016 through Appleford. After 3 miles, turn left on minor road, signed Clifton Hampden. Drive over speed humps in Long Wittenham and at end of village, turn right on minor road, signed Little Wittenham. Fol-low narrow minor road and at T-junction, turn right uphill to car park for the Sinodun Hills and Wittenham Clumps.

Drop downhill and turn left on minor road to reach T-junction with A4130. Turn left, and at roundabout, go straight over into Wallingford (change to map 175). From centre of town, head north on A329, (back on original map), cross the river at Shillingford and at roundabout, turn left onto A423. After one mile, turn left to reach Dorchester. Drive through village, turning left on minor road to reach A415. Turn left through Clifton Hampden and continue on A415 to return to Abingdon.

APPROX DISTANCE: 27 MILES

RECOMMENDED:

Plenty of choice in Abingdon, Wallingford and Dorchester on Thames; Red Lion, The Wheatsheaf, Drayton; The Swan, George & Dragon, The Fish, Sutton Courtenay; Carpenter's Arms, Appleford; The Plough, The Vine, Machine Man Inn, Long Wittenham; Shillingford Bridge Hotel, The Kingfisher, Shillingford; Barley Mow Inn, Clifton Hampden.

Our natural starting point is ABINGDON, whose unspoilt riverfront combines with an historic centre of exceptional interest. It owes its origins to the 7th century Benedictine Abbey of St. Mary which, by the 15th century, was considered second only in importance to Glastonbury. Barely a century later, many abbey buildings were demolished in the Dissolution. Remnants such as the gateway, attached to St. Nicholas church off Market Square, the Long Gallery and The Checker only hint at the splendour of Abingdon's monastic past. The Unicorn

Old Gaol, Abingdon

Theatre, together with the Mill Stream Gallery, occupies part of an old abbey building. (Open Tues to Sun, 2.00-4.00. Tel:01235 553701).

Abingdon was once the county town of Berkshire. Over the centuries, many industries have contributed to Abingdon's prosperity including cloth, brewing, agricultural machinery, flour milling and, until the 1970's, MG cars. The old County Hall, described by Pevsner as "the grandest town hall in England" and now a museum, was originally built as the County Assize Court and market house. Constructed in the 17th century by Christopher Kempster, a master mason and pupil of Wren, the hall is a magnificent legacy of that time. (Open all year, Tues-Sun 11.00-5.00, 4.00 in winter. Free admission. Roof open on selected Sundays. Tel: 01235 523703).

St. Helen's church contains a maze of aisles and chapels, each with its own distinctive beauty. In fact, the church is quite an odd

County Hall Museum, Abingdon

shape; its width is greater than its length which causes a moment's disorientation on entering. Within the precincts of the church are three sets of almshouses. The largest is Christ's Hospital, Long Alley, founded by the Guild of the Holy Cross in 1446 with Brick Alley and the quaintly named Twitty's almshouses making up the trio. Beyond the church lies a delightful stretch of river and it's from here that the impressive size of St. Helen's can be appreciated.

Each June, the Election of the Mayor of Ock Street is held, a custom revived in 1938. The new mayor holds office for only one day, during which time he is "danced in" all over Abingdon and vast quantities of food and drink are consumed. During national celebrations, such as royal weddings, it's customary for buns to be thrown onto the local populace from the roof of the County Hall. Perhaps this explains the term 'bunfight'.

As we head towards our first stop, the brooding presence on the right is the modern monstrosity of Didcot Power Station. With some relief we arrive in SUTTON COURTENAY, alongside one of the loveliest reaches of the Thames. The village, full of diverse houses, timber framed, stone and brick, is interspersed with beautiful gardens spread along winding lanes around a spacious green. All Saints church is the burial place of two figures of renown. The former Liberal Prime Minister Herbert Henry Asquith lived out his retirement in the village and was buried in the churchyard in 1928. The author George Orwell lies buried in a simple grave under his real name, Eric Blair.

The idyllic village of LONG WITTENHAM has many appealing features, including cruck cottages, old fishponds, a pigeon-cote, a Saxon cross, the remains of a cockpit and St. Anthony's Well which is reputed to have healing powers. The Norman church of St. Mary's contains a rare lead font which, to prevent it being melted down into bullets for use in the Civil War, was hidden inside a wooden casing. The Pendon Museum houses a model landscape with exquisite representations of the local countryside in the 1930's. Men of all ages will be fascinated by the model railway exhibits. (Open all year, weekends, 2.00-5.00 plus Weds in July/August and bank holidays 11.00-5.00. Admission charge. Tel: 01865 407365).

We head now for the Sinodun Hills which although not particularly high, dominate the surrounding, much gentler, countryside. The views across the river are outstanding, out of all proportion to the effort needed to climb them. WITTENHAM CLUMPS is a most unromantic name for a magical spot where Iron Age and Roman artefacts have been unearthed, a legacy of the formidable fort which once occupied the summit of one of the hills.

WALLINGFORD originally developed at the point where the Icknield Way forded the river Thames and to guard the approaches an 11th century castle was built, which enjoyed a long and proud history. The Empress Matilda and her son, later Henry II, made Wallingford a stronghold for their forces and the town saw the end of this 12th century civil war when the Treaty of Wallingford was signed here. Centuries later, in another, more famous, Civil War, Wallingford was the last Royalist town in the country, and the castle withstood a siege for 65 days, before it fell to Cromwell. From the earthworks, and scattered ruins in Castle Gardens, lovely views extend across Wallingford to the Downs beyond.

At one time, Wallingford was the largest town in Wessex and even had its own mint. Little remains of the mediaeval town, most of the current buildings dating from the 17th and 18th centuries. The Wallingford Museum takes the visitor on a jour-

Ruins of Wallingford Castle

Ruins of Wallingford Castle

ney from Saxon to mediaeval times. (Open March to November, Tues to Fri 2.00-5.00, Sat 10.30-5.00 plus Suns & bank holidays from June to August, 2.00-5.00. Admission charge. Tel: 01491 835065). Three churches remain. The flint St. Mary's was rebuilt in the 19th century and the oldest is St. Leonard's which retains some Saxon work. The now redundant St. Peter's boasts an octagonal lantern with a hollow spire rising into the sky.

The picturesque village of DORCHESTER ON THAMES nestles in glorious countryside by the Thames. The Saxons founded a cathedral here in 635AD, which became the cathedral of Wessex. By the 9th century, Dorchester was the focus of a huge Mercian diocese whose influence stretched from the Humber to the Thames but, by the Norman conquest, the bishopric had moved to Lincoln. During the early 12th century, the Augustinians began construction of the Abbey Church of St. Peter and St. Paul on the site of the cathedral. This magnificent structure remains a striking reminder of the town's past importance. The huge sanctuary windows are remarkable for their combination of window tracery and stained glass. The unusual statue of a crusader, Sir John Holcombe, lies in

Tomb of Sir John Holcombe, Abbey Church of St Peter and St Paul, Dorchester on Thames

High Street, Dorchester on Thames

the Lady Chapel. Unlike many static monuments, he is caught in the act of drawing a sword. Take a look at the 14th century "monks' corbel" on the pier near the lead font. The carving shows a group of dozing monks, oblivious to the higher matters of divine office they should have been observing. The only part of the monastery buildings to survive is the guesthouse which now houses the fascinating Abbey Museum. (Open Easter weekend, April and Oct, weekends. May to Sept, Tues to Sat 10.30-6.00, Suns and bank holidays, 2.00-6.00. Free admission. Tel: 01865 340056).

A walk along a jumble of meandering lanes branching off the High Street reveals a charming blend of thatched cottages, timber framed buildings with overhanging storeys and stone houses. If the fancy takes you, follow a footpath across fields to the place where the river Thame joins the Thames. Two rivers confusingly spelt alike, but pronounced quite differently. The former rhymes with "name" while the latter is of course pronounced "Tems". What a wonderfully dotty language we have! On the return journey, as you pass Clifton Hampden, you can divert to the Barley Mow Inn, made famous by Jerome K. Jerome in his book, *Three Men in a Boat*.

FURTHER EXPLORATION:

Space precludes the mention of every village in Oxfordshire worth a visit. What follows is very much a personal choice. The charm of the showpiece village of GREAT TEW is enhanced by a mix of thatched cottages. (Map 164, 395293). EAST HENDRED, east of Wantage, (map 174, 460885), contains outstanding examples of cruck cottages, Georgian plasterwork and Tudor brick.

EWELME (map 164, 645915) has been described as one of the loveliest villages in Oxfordshire, earning fame for its watercress beds, almshouses and school. Its splendid church, St. Mary's, is very reminiscent of East Anglia with brick battlements, squared stones and flint. Inside, the tombs are rightly famous, in particular the magnificent tomb of Alice, Duchess of Suffolk and granddaughter of Geoffrey Chaucer. On her left arm is the Order of the Garter, an unusual decoration for a woman of the 15th century. Thomas Chaucer, the poet's son, lies in St. John's Chapel and Jerome K. Jerome is buried in the churchyard.

BLEWBURY (map 174, 532858), is best appreciated on foot. The brook winds through the village amid timbered buildings and thatched cottages. The elegant village of BAMPTON (map 164, 314033) remains a stronghold of Morris dancing. An annual festival brings hundreds of visitors each year and each Whit Monday an event called the Great Shirt Race is held, commemorating the day in 784 AD when the wonderfully named Ethelred the Shirtless pursued villagers in search of his clothes.

8. COME ALL TO CHURCH

(A.E. Housman)

Oxfordshire is blessed with an astonishing variety of churches containing outstanding examples of brass, mediaeval wall paintings and elaborate memorials. The Normans bequeathed various crypts, windows, arches and doorways as reminders of this striking period in ecclesiastical architecture. During the middle ages, the wealth generated by the wool trade enabled grand parish churches to be built. These contrast with the humble country church whose very simplicity and peaceful reverence is, in its own way, more moving than any ostentation.

One of the most fascinating aspects of visiting churches is that until you open the door and walk inside, you never know what to expect. The humblest exterior can hide the most elaborate interior, and the grandest edifice often reveals how all the money has been spent while the inside can be quite ordinary.

A church provides a great sense of continuity in any town or village and you will find generations of the same family remembered on tombs and headstones. Churches are beginning to recognise the importance of the casual visitor who may come as much to see interesting memorials or architecture as for any religious belief. In these sad times of vandalism and theft, not all churches can risk being left open every day but there is usually a notice in the porch indicating the whereabouts of the key holder.

It would be easy to spend many days criss-crossing the county visiting every church of note. Our tour is more modest in scope and is centred on Thame. I hope you will find it a fascinating pilgrimage and that you'll make a generous contribution in each church as the cost of upkeep is prohibitive.

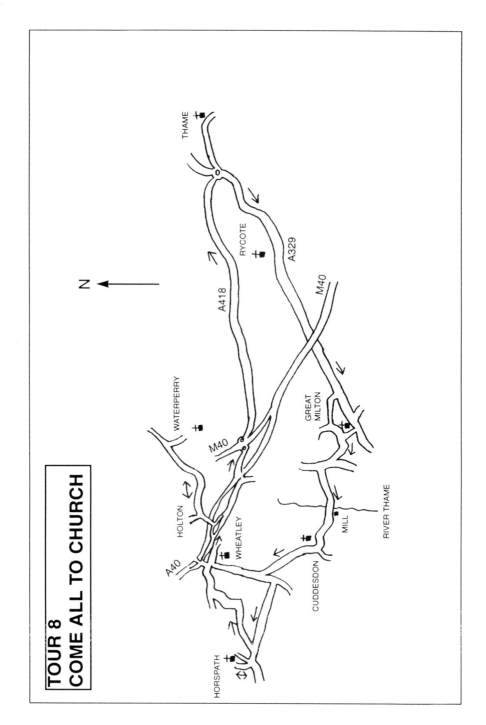

TOUR 8
COME ALL TO CHURCH

N

THAME

RYCOTE

A329

A418

M40

WATERPERRY

M40

GREAT
MILTON

HOLTON

A40

WHEATLEY

RIVER THAME

MILL

CUDDESDON

HORSPATH

64

DIRECTIONS: (OS MAPS 164, 165)

Head south west from Thame on A329 (change to map 164), and go over M40. 2 miles further on, take the second turning on the right for Great Milton. Go past the church and after a sharp bend, take the first left onto a narrow lane, signed Cuddesdon. At a T-junction, turn right and very shortly left on a narrow, muddy lane. Cross the river Thame by Cuddesdon Mill and climb to Cuddesdon village. At T-junction, turn right, signed Wheatley and at another T-junction, turn left and after a quarter of a mile mile, turn right, signed Horspath.

Go under the old railway bridge and just past pub, turn right and immediately right again to reach the church in Horspath. Return to junction by pub and turn left, back under the bridge and almost immediately turn left, signed Littleworth. Drive uphill and through Littleworth and at T-junction, turn right, signed Wheatley. Drive straight through Wheatley, past church and at T-junction, turn right and immediately left. Turn left again past Holton, go over M40 and turn right to reach Waterperry. Return to junction in Wheatley and turn left. Turn left again and after 1 mile join A418, crossing double roundabout over M40 (back on original map) to return to Thame.

APPROX DISTANCE: 22 MILES

RECOMMENDED:

Ample choice in Thame; King's Head, Great Milton; The Plough, Great Haseley; Bat & Ball, Cuddesdon; Chequers Inn, Queen's Head, Horspath; Cricketers Arms, Littleworth; The Sun, King's Arms, Wheatley; Tea Shop, Waterperry Gardens.

We start from the attractive, market town of THAME, full of life and bustle. The long High Street reveals houses and shops of every hue and style, together with an amazing number of pubs. The timber framed almshouses and tithe barn near the church are typical examples of Thame's striking architecture. The Bird Cage Inn, a quaint timber framed pub, has at various times throughout its history been a prison and a leper house. At one time, a thief known as the "Magpie" was imprisoned here whereupon locals said "the bird is in his cage" and the name for the pub was born.

The welcoming St. Mary's church is known chiefly for its magnificent array of monuments and windows, in a variety of styles. The superb south porch gives the first hint of the wonders inside. Monuments to the Williams and Quartremain families dominate, in particular the tomb of Lord Williams and his wife Elizabeth which occupies the centre of the chancel. In the 15th century, Richard Quartremain was councillor to Richard, Duke of York and later his son, Edward IV. He was also the builder of Rycote Chapel which is our next destination.

At the end of a bumpy lane lies the chapel of St. Michael and All Angels at RYCOTE, which contains striking pews which practically block the chancel. One has a minstrels' gallery and the other an

Tomb of Lord Williams, St Mary's Church, Thame

Ottoman style canopy, both with beautifully carved screens. Another pew enjoys the luxury of a fireplace and a superb blue painted ceiling studded with gold stars. Overlying all this is the wagon-vaulted roof, a further remarkable feature of this small place of worship. Over the years, Rycote has seen many royal visitors, including Elizabeth I, James I and Charles I. A massive yew tree outside supposedly came from the Garden of Gethsemane and there is a tale of a 12th century bishop visiting the Holy Land. The tree is certainly ancient, so perhaps there's a grain of truth in the story. Should you see a tall woman on your visit, take careful note of where she goes. If she passes through the hedge, you may have seen the resident ghost. (Open March to end Sept, Fri to Sun and bank holidays, 2.00-6.00. Admission charge. Tel: English Heritage Regional Office 0117 9750700).

We move on to GREAT MILTON, where St. Peter's displays a blend of architectural styles. Designed to be portable, the marble

Rycote Chapel

altar was taken to parishioners' homes when they were too ill to attend services. A case of "have altar, will travel" perhaps? Under a gilded canopy, the alabaster figures of Sir Michael Dormer, Lord Mayor of London, his wife and father, lie on a marble tomb. The edifice boasts a rich feast of decorated work with heraldic shields and intricate marble reliefs. Next to the church, is an elegant manor house whose historical credentials date back to the 13th century. It is now occupied by a famous French restaurant, for which you will need bottomless pockets.

We now climb to CUDDESDON, where the view from All Saints church spreads far across the plain of Oxford to the Chilterns. Inside the Norman doorway you'll find an elaborately gilded high altar, carved tower arches and an east window by Kempe. The side windows depict the coats of arms of various Bishops of Oxford, reflecting the church's close links with the nearby Anglican Theological College, founded in 1854.

The modern village of HORSPATH shelters a delightful church, dedicated to the patron saint of cripples and beggars, St. Giles. Note especially the stained glass window commemorating an Oxford don who defended himself from a wild boar by thrusting a volume of Aristotle down the beast's throat, with the words "Graecum est",

Lychgate and All Saints Church, Cuddesdon

which roughly translated means "With the compliments of the Greeks". Certainly a 'novel' defence! The attack occurred on nearby Shotover Hill, although today's walkers are unlikely to encounter anything quite so fierce as a wild boar.

During the 13th century, while it was the property of Abingdon Abbey, WHEATLEY was much smaller than it is today and was considered a satellite of Cuddesdon, a situation now reversed. One of the most unusual features of the village is the lock-up, a pyramid-shaped stone building used to incarcerate drunks before they were sent to the court at Oxford.

We divert slightly off our route to visit WATERPERRY, where the gardens and St. Mary's church occupy the grounds of a Georgian House. The 83 acres include such delights as the Alpine Nursery, Virgin's Walk, the Rose, Rock and Formal Gardens. One of the glories of the garden is almost 100 yards of herbaceous perennials, designed to provide a profusion of colour during the summer. (Gardens - open April to Oct, 10.00-5.30, Nov to March, 10.00-5.00. Admission charge. Tel: 01844 339254). The church is all weird angles with strangely shaped roofs and a wooden belfry, extremely rare in Oxfordshire and more reminiscent of the Teme valley in Worcestershire.

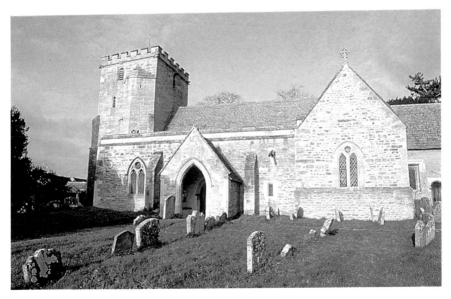

St Giles Church, Horspath

Stone carving, St Mary's Church, Wheatley

FURTHER EXPLORATION:

Again, this is a personal choice and barely touches on all the churches you can explore. St. Mary the Virgin, IFFLEY, in south Oxford, is a fine Norman church with a font large enough for any newly christened infant to swim a couple of laps of honour.

Near the entrance to the churchyard of St. Andrew's, ODDINGTON (map 164, 554150) is the grave of a Maori Princess. Margaret Staple Brown, neé Papakura, died in 1930 and many New Zealand visitors come to pay their respects. St. Mary's in BLOXHAM (map 151, 430360), of almost cathedral-like proportions, contains incredible carvings of the Last Judgement, 13th century arches and the delicate Milcombe Chapel.

The chief glory of England's smallest cathedral, Christ Church in OXFORD, is the Becket Window which commemorates the murder of the 12th century saint. Another outstanding example of workmanship is the Jonah Window by van Linge, complete with Jonah and the gourd tree but minus the whale.

9. MOTHER NATURE

Oxfordshire has no large areas of wilderness. Pockets of chalk downland, woodland and river valleys survive amid an arable landscape. Pressures of road construction, building development and the ravages of modern pesticide-driven farming exact a heavy toll on our countryside. Farmland birds are decreasing as their habitats are sprayed to squeeze as much production out of the land as possible. Hedgerows, which once formed valuable wildlife corridors, are grubbed out or flail-mown to death. On our Tour, the proximity of a works at Chinnor and the M40 slicing through Aston Rowant Nature Reserve offer uncomfortable reminders of the pressures our countryside faces. The designation of some precious habitats as nature reserves is often the only way to provide protection.

Our Tour nudges into the Chilterns, whose beechwoods are breathtakingly beautiful in the autumn. For the naturalist, woodland is at its best during spring and early summer, when birds are at their most active. Pay a visit early in the morning to appreciate the wonder of a woodland dawn chorus, with every bird trying to out-sing its neighbour, stake out a territory and attract a mate. Close views of wildlife require a little effort and patience, together with a slice of luck. Binoculars are a vital aid to identification and pocket books on birds, flowers and trees will prove immensely helpful.

The Berkshire, Buckinghamshire and Oxfordshire Naturalists' Trust (BBONT) protects many woodland, grassland, heathland and wetland sites and relies heavily on its membership, donations and the hard work of volunteers. Membership details are available from 3, Church Cowley Road, Oxford OX4 3JR, tel: 01865 775476.

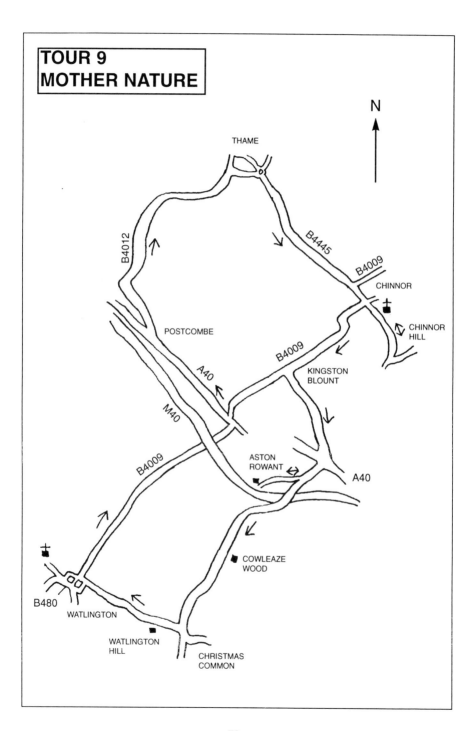

TOUR 9
MOTHER NATURE

N

THAME

B4012

B4445

B4009

CHINNOR

CHINNOR
HILL

POSTCOMBE

B4009

A40

KINGSTON
BLOUNT

M40

ASTON
ROWANT

A40

B4009

COWLEAZE
WOOD

B480

WATLINGTON

WATLINGTON
HILL

CHRISTMAS
COMMON

DIRECTIONS: (OS MAPS 165, 175)

Leave Thame on B4445 to Chinnor village. Continue up hill on Bledlow Ridge Road. Access to the Chinnor Hill reserve is by Hilltop Lane (grid ref 766005). Return to Chinnor village and turn left on B4009. At Kingston Blount, turn left on minor road uphill, signed Kingston Grove. At A40, turn left and immediately right on minor road, signed Christmas Common. After half a mile, at start of conifer wood, turn right on unsigned road to Aston Rowant National Nature Reserve.

Return to junction, and turn right on minor road over M40 and after a mile, look for car park for Cowleaze Wood on left. Continue on minor road, then turn right at Christmas Common, signed Watlington. Within half a mile, watch for car park on Watlington Hill on left.

Continue downhill and follow one way system into Watlington. Turn right at T-junction onto B480, and shortly right on B4009, signed M40. Go under the M40 and turn left on A40. After Postcombe, turn right on B4012 to return to Thame.

APPROX DISTANCE: 23 MILES

RECOMMENDED:

Plenty of choice in Thame; The Crown, The Black Boy, The Red Lion, Chinnor; Cherry Tree, Kingston Blount; Fox & Hounds, Christmas Common; Carriers Arms, Fox & Hounds, Watlington; Leathern Bottle, Lewknor; Lambert Arms, A40; The Feathers, Postcombe.

As with the previous Tour, we start from Thame but then head immediately towards CHINNOR HILL, where you can enjoy glorious views. Beech woodland dominates this BBONT reserve, interspersed with areas of scrub and chalk grassland which support plants such as autumn gentian.

Beginning at Goring by the Thames, the 50 mile ridge of chalk which forms the backbone of the Chilterns crosses this southern corner of Oxfordshire. The hills present a steep, west facing escarpment which slopes away gently to the east. Interspersed with valleys and grassy downs, the hills are criss-crossed by numerous footpaths and bridleways, including the Ridgeway. The Chiltern woodlands were chosen as part of the release scheme for that magnificent bird of prey, the red kite. Despite continuing persecution, the red kite population is generally increasing every year. I shall never forget the time we saw three of these majestic birds circling in the air at the same time, with their forked tails obvious even at a distance and the rusty red colouring on their wings catching the sun. Such agility and mastery of the air was a thrilling sight.

We continue to the National Nature Reserve at ASTON ROWANT. A well-marked nature trail, offering superb views, explores acres of chalk grassland, scrub and beechwood and sup-

Aston Rowant Nature Reserve, Chilterns

ports an amazing variety of flora, including 126 species of plants. The close grazing of rabbits and sheep maintains the grassland and produces typical downland plants which glory in exotic names such as sheep's fescue, salad burnet, horseshoe vetch and glaucous sedge, to name but a few. Growing on the denser turf are more familiar flowers such as oxeye daisy, marjoram orchid and kidney vetch.

The scrub is a glorious tangle of ash, blackthorn, bramble, buckthorn, juniper, wild privet and spindle. The woodland on Beacon Hill is a mix of beech, hawthorn, whitebeam, yew and elder and in places is too thick to allow light through, although this doesn't affect plants such as white and violet helleborine which can survive the shade. In the clearings, bluebells, yellow archangel, woodruff, guelder rose and wood melick may be seen and in the autumn, the beech trees exhibit a magnificent display of colour.

Aston Rowant also supports a diverse range of butterflies including the rare silver spotted skipper, a species only found in the southern chalk landscape. Dingy and grizzled skipper, together with chalkhill blue and dark green fritillary are just a few of the dozens of species, both scarce and common, which thrive on these slopes. Pay a visit in summer and you'll be enthralled as hundreds of these delicate creatures dance through the air.

Birdwatchers too will find much to hold their interest in these woods and scrubland. Healthy populations of nuthatch, treecreeper, woodpecker, kestrel and sparrowhawk thrive, together with the elusive, and rare, hawfinch. This striking, bulky bird shows a particular fondness for hornbeam trees but is very wary and easily disturbed. It's more likely you'll hear its distinctive "zik" call as it feeds high up in the tree canopy. The scrub provides a valuable habitat for many species of insects and birds. From its position on the edge of the Chiltern escarpment, Aston Rowant can be a wonderful place for seeing bird migration in full swing. During spring, birds such as wheatears, whinchats and ring ouzels may rest here.

Breeding birds include summer visitors such as blackcap, garden warbler, chiffchaff, willow warbler and whitethroat along with the more common tit and finch families. During the winter, the berry rich scrub and hedges provide essential food for redwing and fieldfare, members of the thrush family which arrive from Scandinavia to take advantage of the UK's milder winters. Careful scanning with binoculars among the foraging flocks of finches may, with luck, reveal small numbers of siskin and redpoll, together with the much rarer brambling. The proximity of the M40 means that blinkers and a set of ear-plugs could be useful for one half of the nature trail - or you could follow the birds' example and ignore it!

A short distance further on, watch for signs to the Chiltern Sculpture Trail in COWLEAZE WOOD. Managed by the Forestry Commission, the 70 acres are a mixture of conifer and broadleaved trees. A waymarked sculpture trail

Sculpture Trail, Cowleaze Wood, the Chilterns

winds through the trees revealing some startling apparitions. New, mostly contemporary sculptures are commissioned each year, some designed to be permanent additions, others purely temporary which will either be removed or degrade back into the forest. The subjects chosen may not be everyone's cup of tea but they are certainly memorable. Personally, I find more fascination in the natural world than anything crafted by mankind, but you must make up your own mind.

We pass through the curiously named hamlet of Christmas Common, so called because in 1643, a temporary truce was declared by the Royalists and the Parliamentarians to allow both sides to celebrate Christmas. Then we plunge down the 700 foot escarpment of WATLINGTON HILL. Protected by the National Trust, it shelters many examples of flora native to chalk grassland and the beech woodland provides excellent habitat for breeding birds such as robins, mistle thrushes, coal tits and goldcrests. The woods play

Squirrel

Cowleaze Wood, the Chilterns

host to a breathtaking display of bluebells each spring.

The small town of WATLINGTON, with its narrow, meandering streets, huddles at the foot of Watlington Hill. The Domesday Book recorded the existence of five mills here when the land was held by Preaux Abbey and the D'Oilly barons. The mills and a later castle have disappeared, while the once numerous inns are much reduced in number.

FURTHER EXPLORATION:

The ancient fen of OTMOOR (map 164) north east of Oxford, is an eerie, atmospheric place. The 4,000 acres, where the river Ray and its tributary streams form a wetland habitat, are of immense importance to wildlife, including many rare species of butterflies, birds and plants. However, this marshy wilderness has little protection and much has been drained for use as farmland. At the time of writing, the RSPB are attempting to raise funds to buy much of the area to protect its future as a wetland reserve. This would form an important link in the chain of similar habitats across the Midlands, which prove invaluable for migrating birds. For the sake of the wildlife, let's hope they succeed. Equip yourself with binoculars and follow footpaths across Otmoor, but beware of the rifle range!

A BBONT reserve, WARBURG, north of Henley (map 175, 720881), is a magnificent example of ancient woodland, scrub and chalk grassland. From the visitors' centre, follow public footpaths and a nature trail and you may see some of the 300 recorded species of flora, together with abundant bird and animal life. East of Oxford, SHOTOVER COUNTRY PARK is a remnant of a Royal forest where the woods, heath, grassland and scrub shelter a rich variety of wildlife.

10. STATELY HOMES

Oxfordshire lays claim to a tremendous variety of historic houses, ranging from unpretentious manors to the grandiose splendour of Blenheim Palace. The number of imposing country mansions which remain as family homes is shrinking each year. Many houses have become elegant country hotels or have been divided into apartments. Other owners have welcomed tourists to survive, opening their houses and gardens to visitors. Some organise shows, weddings, conferences and other country events, while others provide tempting teashops which can attract people who would otherwise never dream of wandering around a stately home.

Many of Oxfordshire's country houses are in the care of the National Trust and English Heritage and some of the larger houses open for a considerable part of the year, many as early as March through to October. Others may open only for a few weekends in the summer. I've listed the current details for each property but it's always best to check in advance on the opening dates and times in order to avoid a wasted journey.

It goes without saying that some properties can be very crowded at weekends during the summer or at bank holidays. If you can't manage a midweek visit but don't like traipsing round a house in a queue more reminiscent of a supermarket, try to choose a weekend during spring or autumn.

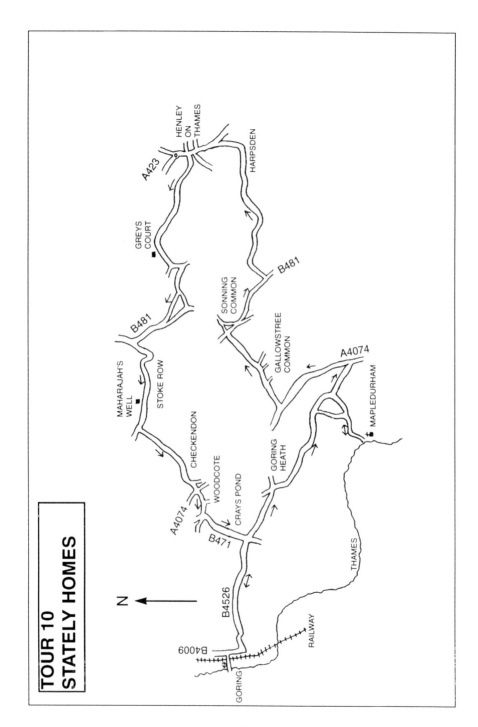

TOUR 10
STATELY HOMES

DIRECTIONS: (OS MAP 175)

From Henley's main street, go up Market Place, to left of Information Centre, uphill on minor road. After 3 miles, reach Greys Court on right. Turn right from Greys Court, follow road as it bends right, following signs for Shepherds Green. At junction, turn right on B481, signed Nettlebed, and after 1 mile, turn left on minor road, signed Stoke Row. Use Stoke Row village hall car park to visit Maharajah's Well.

Take first left turning, signed Checkendon. Ignore side turnings, and drive through Checkendon to join A4074. Turn right and immediately left on minor road. At crossroads, turn left on B471 through Woodcote. At crossroads, turn right on B4526 and at T-junction, turn right on B4009 and take first left to Goring. Return to B4009 and turn right. Take first left, on B4526 and go straight through earlier crossroads at Crays Pond on B4526.

After two miles, bear right on minor road, signed Goring Heath. Ignore side turnings, and after 3 miles, turn right on minor road, signed Mapledurham. Return to junction, and turn right to reach A4074. Turn left, signed Oxford. After 3 miles, by pub, turn right through Gallowstree Common. Continue to T-junction and turn right, signed Sonning Common. Shortly reach crossroads, go straight over, signed Shiplake and after 1 mile, turn left on minor road signed Harpsden. Follow minor road through Harpsden, bending left to return to Henley.

APPROX DISTANCE: 29 MILES

RECOMMENDED:

Plenty of choice in Henley on Thames and Goring; Tea room, Grey's Court; The Lamb Inn, Saltwell; Crooked Billet, Cherry Tree, Stoke Row; White Lion, Crays Pond; King Charles Head, Goring Heath; Old Manor Tea Rooms, Mapledurham House; Packhorse Inn, Chazey Heath; The Fox, Cane End; Greyhound, Rotherfield Peppard; Butchers Arms, Sonning Common.

Famous for its regatta, the market town of HENLEY ON THAMES belongs more to the Chilterns commuter belt than the Heart of England. Once a river port, Henley developed into an important staging post on the coach route between London and Oxford. The large number of inns which still survive are a legacy of that time. Thousands of visitors come to Henley to enjoy the Royal Regatta in early July while the Town Regatta takes place at the end of the month. Henley's position is truly beautiful, alongside one of the loveliest stretches of the Thames, with attractive buildings from every period clustered along the waterfront. Temple Island, surrounded by unspoilt meadows, was built in 1771 as a summer house for Fawley Court. Needless to say, during the summer, Henley is crammed full of boats of every size and description. The photogenic Henley Bridge, with carved heads of Father Thames and Isis, replaced an earlier bridge in 1786.

Henley's wealth of historical buildings are a fascinating mixture, with fine examples of half timbering, stockbroker brick and Georgian elegance. The upper storey of Chantry House, possibly the oldest building in the town, is timber framed and contains a long aisled room, divided by piers. St. Mary's church boasts an exterior

Paddle steamer, Henley on Thames

Maharajah's Well, Stoke Row village near Henley on Thames

Statue of elephant, Maharajah's Well, Stoke Row village near Henley on Thames

of flint and stone and the tower is crowned by pinnacles. The interior houses a monument to Lady Periam, Francis Bacon's sister, who founded a school in Henley for poor boys. Due to open in 1998 at Mill Meadows is the River and Rowing Museum, which will celebrate the olympic sport of rowing and the town's history. (Tel: 01491 415600).

We leave Henley for our first port of call, the National Trust property of GREYS COURT. Originally built in the 12th century by the Archbishop of York, the current flint and brick gabled Tudor house, built by the Knollys family, incorporates part of the original fortified house. Following extensive and sympathetic restorations, the house and grounds were given to the National Trust in 1968 by Sir Felix Brunner, whose family had occupied the Court since 1937. The beautiful gardens are delightful and feature the Archbishop's Maze, inspired by Robert Runcie's sermon on becoming Archbishop of Canterbury. (Garden open daily except Thurs/Sun, 2.00-6.00. House open March to end Sept, Mon, Weds and Fri 2.00-6.00. Garden - daily except Thurs and Sun 2.00-6.00. Admission charge. Tel: 01491 628529).

MAHARAJAH'S WELL is a most exotic feature of the tranquil

Clock, Village Hall, Goring

rural backwater of Stoke Row village and was a gift from the Maharajah of Benares in 1863, in honour of his friend, Edward Reade of Ipsden House. The well, with its Oriental dome, was dug through the chalk entirely by hand and its depth exceeds the height of St. Paul's Cathedral.

Our halfway point is the delightful village of GORING. The first toll bridge was built just over a hundred years ago to replace the ferry. The Great Western Railway passes through the Goring Gap on its way to Didcot and this, together with its proximity to the Thames, ensured that Goring developed rapidly. However, it remains an unspoilt, pleasant riverside settlement with many attractive buildings. An interesting legend is connected to the Miller of Mansfield Inn. As you can see from the pub sign, the miller had the impudence to serve Henry II a pie containing venison poached from the King's own forest.

Our next destination is the secluded village of MAPLEDURHAM. An intricate network of steep and narrow roads winds down to the river, meaning the village is probably easier to reach by boat than

St Thomas of Canterbury church, Goring

Pub sign, the Miller of Mansfield, Goring

by car. The almshouses, 14th century church and flint cottages slumber in a delightful setting overlooking the river. The clock on St. Margaret's church tower was a present from William IV in 1832 and his initials are stamped on the clockface. In 1588, Mapledurham House was built for the Blount family and contains outstanding collections of furniture and paintings, together with superb examples of plaster ceilings and a fine oak staircase. A private chapel was added in 1797 and is styled entirely in Strawberry Hill Gothic. The house is believed to have been the original inspiration for Kenneth Grahame's Toad Hall, and the BBC used it for their dramatisation of Galsworthy's "The Forsyte Saga". The estate also has literary connections with Alexander Pope and was used in the filming of "The Eagle Has Landed" and more recently for Inspector Morse. Nearby, the restored watermill remains the only surviving working corn and grist mill on the Thames. Flour, ground on the original machinery, can be purchased. (Open Easter to end Sept, weekends and bank holiday mondays, 1.00-5.00 for Mill, 2.30-5.00 for House. Admission charge. Tel: 01189 723350).

FURTHER EXPLORATION:

We have already visited Ashdown House (TOUR 6), Blenheim Palace (TOUR 3), Kingston Bagpuize (TOUR 5) and Rousham House (TOUR 1). The finely proportioned STONOR PARK (map 175, 744893), north of Henley, contains a fascinating collection of paintings, tapestries, sculptures and furniture. An unusual feature in the grounds is a reconstructed stone circle. (Open end March to end Sept, Sun, Bank Holiday Mons, Weds, Thurs, Sat, 2.00-5.30. Admission charge. Tel: 01491 638587).
ARDINGTON HOUSE, near Wantage (map 174, 432882) was built for Edward Clarke in the early 18th century by the Strong family, masons who had previously worked on Blenheim. (Open May to Sept, Mon & bank holidays, 2.30-4.30. Admission charge. Tel: 01235 83324). BUSCOT PARK, near Faringdon (map 163, 245966), is a restored 18th century Adams-style house with gardens. (National Trust. Open March to end Sept, Weds to Fri 2.00-6.00 plus some weekends. Admission charge. Tel: 01367 240786/242094).

The Jacobean CHASTLETON HOUSE, near Chipping Norton, (map 163, 248292) has undergone extensive restoration by the National Trust. Originally built for a wealthy Witney wool merchant and MP, Walter Jones, Chastleton has remained remarkably unchanged through the years and retains many of the original features. (Restricted opening. Limited numbers by pre-booked tickets only. Tel: 01608 674284 for dates and times).

ACKNOWLEDGEMENTS

Thanks are due to Celia Sterne of English Heritage for the pictures of Rycote Chapel, Uffington White Horse, Minster Lovell Hall and North Leigh Roman Villa. My husband Rex, for his support and invaluable help on the manuscript. Unsung local historians who produce informative and entertaining church guides and the helpful staff of the county's Tourist Information Centres.

S. B. Publications produce a wide range of local interest books.
For a catalogue please write to:
S. B. Publications, 19 Grove Road, Seaford, East Sussex BN25 1TP

TOURIST INFORMATION CENTRES IN
OXFORDSHIRE

ABINGDON
8 Market Place   ·
Tel: 01235 522711

BANBURY
Banbury Museum
8 Horsefair
Tel: 01295 259855

BURFORD
The Brewery
Sheep Street
Tel: 01993 823558

CHIPPING NORTON
The Guildhall
Goddards Lane
Tel: 01608 644379

* DIDCOT
The Car Park
Station Road
Tel: 01235 813243

* FARINGDON
The Pump House
5 Market Place
Tel: 01367 242191

HENLEY ON THAMES
Town Hall
Market Place
Tel: 01491 578034

OXFORD
The Old School
Gloucester Green
Tel: 01865 726871

THAME
Market House
North Street
Tel: 01844 212834

WALLINGFORD
Town Hall
Tel: 01491 825844

WANTAGE
Vale & Downland Museum
Tel: 01235 760176

WITNEY
Town Hall
Market Square
Tel: 01993 775802

WOODSTOCK
Hensington Road
Tel: 01993 811038

Also West Oxfordshire Tourism
Woodgreen
Witney
Tel: 01993 770281

* Seasonal opening only